Taco-Tastic!

FSC
www.fsc.org
MIX
Paper | Supporting
responsible forestry
FSC® C004800

Published in 2022 by OH! Life
An imprint of Welbeck Non-Fiction Limited, part of Welbeck Publishing Group.
Based in London and Sydney.
www.welbeckpublishing.com

Text © Victoria Elizondo 2022
The author has asserted her moral rights to be identified as the author of this
Work in accordance with the Copyright Designs and Patents Act 1988.

Design © Welbeck Non-Fiction Limited 2022
Photography by Valerie Ayala © Welbeck Non-Fiction Limited 2022
Cover images: Shutterstock/Rawpixel.com (front and spine); © Welbeck
Non-Fiction Limited (back left and right); Unsplash/andrew-valdivia
(back center).

A CIP catalogue record for this book is available from the British Library.

ISBN 978-1-83861-090-6

Associate Publisher: Lisa Dyer
Copyeditor and writer: Theresa Bebbington
Designer: James Pople
Production Controller: Felicity Awdry

Printed and bound in Dubai

10 9 8 7 6 5 4 3 2 1

Taco-¡Tastic!

OVER 60 RECIPES
TO MAKE TACO TUESDAYS
LAST ALL WEEK LONG

VICTORIA ELIZONDO
PHOTOGRAPHS BY VALERIE AYALA

OH!
LIFE

CONTENTS

PREFACE

Being born in Mexico and raised in United States was a complicated situation while I was growing up. I spent many years trying to fit into a new country and a new lifestyle. Once I got older, I realized how much I missed my culture, traditions, and food.

Becoming a chef was the first step to building a bridge to a country I was starting to forget. As a DACA recipient, I was not permitted to leave the country, so I brought Mexico to me. The response was amazing and eventually I dedicated all my time to cooking Mexican food. In order to create this book, I had to go back to my roots. The vibrancy from my culture translated into colorful dishes made with fresh ingredients.

This book is for the average home cook so I decided to reconnect with my favorite dishes from my childhood that my grandma would make for me. Picadillo was one of them. The book is also a consolidation of memories and recipes that I created for my restaurant.

In this book you will find recipes inspired by authentic Mexican cuisine but modified for busy people cooking for themselves and family. Some ingredients may be difficult to find locally for you, but they can be replaced with more accessible ingredients; suggestions are given throughout.

Tacos have essential components: tortilla, protein, salsa, and garnish. They are all important and help create the perfect taco. If you focus too much on the protein and don't use good tortillas, or make a bland salsa, the taco will not be as enjoyable.

Here you will find everything to make your taco experience fun and exciting. In the first chapter there is a range of salsas, from creamy, to citrusy, to spicy! The second chapter shows you how to make your own tortillas as well as some side dishes. After that you will find taco recipes for all occasions and palates, from vegan to seafood, and there's even a final chapter for taco parties, because sharing food is so important to the Mexican community.

Cooking Mexican food is an act of love, passion, and fun. Don't take it too seriously and feel free to adjust recipes to your liking. Not all tacos need to be authentic. You can have fun with ingredients and create fusions. I truly believe that food brings people together; food is also unconsciously part of your deepest memories. Sort of like when you taste something similar to what you used to eat as a child and you start to remember random things about your childhood. My wish is that you enjoy this book as much I enjoyed writing it.

"I love cooking with vibrant ingredients that represent how colorful Mexican culture is. As a DACA recipient, not being able to go back to my country inspired me to bring Mexico to me and to those around me."

ESSENTIAL INGREDIENTS

While avocado, corn, beans, and rice form the bedrock of Mexican cuisine, a lot of the flavor of local dishes comes from chiles, spices, and herbs. Without them, Mexican food wouldn't be as amazing as it is.

FRESH CHILES

Native to Central America, chiles have been cultivated and used in cooking throughout Mexico since before the Aztecs. There are more than 60 different types of chiles produced in Mexico. Some are smoky, others sweet and floral.

HABANERO: Named after the Cuban city of La Habana (Havana in English), the largest producer is the Yucatán. A lantern-shaped dimpled chile, it is very hot and found most commonly in red, green, or orange, but there are also purple and black versions. It is most similar to a Scotch bonnet. Be very careful when handling.

JALAPEÑO: The name jalapeño is Spanish for "from Xalapa," the capital city of Veracruz, where the pepper was traditionally cultivated. A small, green, mild-to-medium-hot chile used in salsas and sliced as a topping on tacos and burritos, the jalapeño is incredibly versatile and available fresh or pickled.

POBLANO: Dark green, this is the fresh version of the dried chile ancho. It is very mild in heat but hotter when ripe and turning red. Because of its large size, it is often stuffed with cheese and fried.

SERRANO: A small, narrow, medium-hot chile, usually green in color. If you can't locate serrano chiles, you can usually substitute jalapeños, though serranos are spicier. Like jalapeños, they are great roasted or used in salsas and relishes.

DRIED CHILES

Thanks to the dehydration process, we are able to enjoy a wide variety of peppers that, once dried, turn into a completely different color, texture, smell, flavor, and even into a new name. Chipotles, for example, are actually dry jalapeños. Dried chiles are mainly used to turn into a paste to then be added to soups and stews. They can be rehydrated before using by soaking them in hot water, but toasting them before incorporating them into your recipe will highlight their flavor and notes.

ANCHO: Dried poblano, this is one of the most used peppers in Mexican cuisine. It is rich and robust with a mild to hot spice level.

CHILE DE ÁRBOL: Four times hotter than the jalapeño and almost one-quarter of its size, this small and nutty bright red pepper is commonly used to bring spice to salsas, stews, or any other dish that needs an extra kick.

CHIPOTLE: A small smoke-dried jalapeño with a smoky, sweet, and spicy flavor. Perfect for making adobo sauce and marinates. It is used in both Mexican and Tex-Mex cuisine.

GUAJILLO: Large and bright red, this mild chile has sweet and smoky flavors. Choose those that are smooth and shiny.

MORITA: Like chipotles, these are also smoke-dried red jalapeños. Morita chiles are technically a variation of the chipotle pepper.

PASILLA: A dark, wrinkly dried chile with a fruity flavor, this has medium hotness and is often used in stews and sauces. *Pasilla* means "little raisin" as it has a similar texture to the fruit.

HERBS AND SPICES

The key herbs and spices you will need are discussed below, but it's worth mentioning *hierbas de olor*, a mix of thyme, marjoram, bay, and oregano, often sold in bundles in markets.

CHILE POWDER: Look out for specific chile powders, such as those labeled ancho, pasilla, habanero, guajillo, or de árbol, each with their own specific flavor profile.

CILANTRO (CORIANDER): A key ingredient in Mexican cuisine, fresh cilantro is crisp and fresh. When dried, it adds a more subtle, herbal flavor to a dish.

CUMIN: Mexico adopted this fragrant spice from the Mediterranean. When using cumin, you must be careful not to use too much. Less is better due to its depth and earthy and warm flavor.

EPAZOTE: A pungent culinary herb used mostly in the southern region of Mexico, the flavor is so unique, a combination of mint, pine, anise, and oregano. This herb is carminative, which means that it can help reduce digestive gas brought on from beans. Although there is no real substitute, you can use dried oregano.

MEXICAN OREGANO: Used in numerous Mexican dishes to add an earthy taste, this is a bright, pungent, and aromatic herb. It is not to be confused with Italian oregano, which is a different plant altogether. Mexican oregano is from the verbena family, and there are several strains, however the Italian herb is often substituted in recipes.

STORECUPBOARD INGREDIENTS

There are so many Mexican ingredients that you can keep stocked in your pantry, from purées, pastes, and condiments to nuts, seeds, rice, and beans, but here are some of the essentials.

ACHIOTE PASTE: Made with annatto seeds, garlic, spices, and vinegar, the red paste adds not only flavor but a bright color.

BEANS (FRIJOLES): Available dried or canned, dried are preferable, though you will need to cook them from scratch.

CHIPOTLES IN ADOBO: As it is difficult to find chipotles (dried jalapeños) outside Mexico, use the can or jar versions, which are rehydrated with tomato purée, vinegar, garlic, and other spices.

GARLIC AND ONIONS: Available fresh, in a jar, or as a powder, garlic is a key ingredient in Mexican food, as are onions, which are used raw or as onion powder.

MOLE POBLANO PASTE: This chocolate chile paste is a perfect mix of sweet and spicy and makes a wonderful sauce for chicken or served in dishes.

PINTO BEANS (FRIJOLES PINTOS): The pale speckled bean is traditionally cooked in a pot as *frijoles de la Olla*, mashed and fried, added to stews or used to fill tacos, tostadas, and burritos.

RICE: A staple food, rice is often cooked with broth and tomatoes to make red rice, or with parsley and chiles as a green rice, or as plain white rice. It is include in different beverages as well, such as the sweet milky drink *horchata*.

SALSA INGLESA: The Mexican version of Worcestershire sauce, this fermented blend of vinegar, molasses, chile, soy sauce, tamarind, anchovies, garlic, and cloves is used as a flavor enhancer and meat marinade.

CREAM AND CHEESE

Commonly used as topping or garnish, some Mexican cheeses such as quesillo can be melted in quesadillas or stuffed in peppers.

CREMA: A tangy condiment, crema is similar to sour cream or crème fraîche but richer, and made with lime and salt. It is used to top tacos, soups, and other Mexican food.

COTIJA: A white cheese that is salty and milky. When young, it is most similar to feta; aged it is more like Parmesan. It is often used crumbled or grated over tacos, soups, or salads and softens when heated but doesn't melt. Feta or Lancashire cheese can be used as a substitute.

QUESILLO: Also known as Oaxaca cheese, this is a white semi-hard cheese similar in texture to mozzarella (which can be substituted).

QUESO FRESCO: Translating as "fresh cheese," this mild white cheese is light and salty-sour. It is made from cow's milk or cow's and goat's, with rennet, lemon juice, or vinegar added. Feta can be substituted but it should be soaked in water first to reduce its salty tanginess.

FRESH PRODUCE

In Mexico it is possible to grow an abundant variety of fresh fruit and vegetables, which makes their local markets—and many in the Southwest of the U.S.—exceptional for seasonal ingredients. For the freshest produce, seek out your local farmer's market.

AVOCADO: Called the "green gold of Mexico," this fruit is most popular in guacamole but also used in salsas, sauces, soups, as toppings, and in desserts.

CALABACITAS (ZUCCHINI/COURGETTE): Although you can substitute the American or European counterpart, the Mexican calabacitas is a little different, with a more pear-like shape, a denser flesh, and a lighter or more speckled outer skin.

CORN: Like chiles, there are many varieties of corn, over 50 types. Even though Mexico gets their yellow corn from the United States, the most popular to eat is the white corn. It is dried and ground to make masa harina for tortillas but is also included in beverages such as *atole* (a hot drink sweetened with vanilla and cinnamon), *champurrado* (hot chocolate), and *tejuino* (a cold fermented drink).

JÍCAMA: Also known as the Mexican turnip or yam bean, this starchy root vegetable is closest to a sweet potato in flavor and

texture. It is juicy rather than starchy, and is delicious eaten raw. It is traditionally eaten peeled in chunks or strips with lime juice and chile powder.

LIMES: Mexico has been the world's largest producer and exporter of limes since the 1950s, and the lime—or *limón*—is a key flavor in many dishes and drinks, as well as served as wedges with meals.

NOPALES (CACTUS): The flesh of the Opuntia cactus, prickly pear, this is best when bought fresh, though jarred and canned nopales are available from Mexican suppliers and online. They have a slightly tart flavor and are used in tacos, salads, and as a side dish.

PINEAPPLE: Pineapples are grown along the tropical coasts and in the Papaloapan River lowlands of Veracruz and Oaxaca. Loma Bonita in Oaxaca calls itself the Pineapple Capital of the World. Popular in salsas, drinks, and with chicken, pork, and fish, pineapple is also found candied and in sweet tamales for sale at Mexican fairs.

TOMATILLOS: These green fruits have a papery husk and, although related to the tomato, are not green tomatoes. They have a tart citrus flavor that makes them excellent in salsas. Use canned versions if you can't locate them fresh.

TORTILLAS

Tortillas are part of everyday life in Mexico. The are often used as utensils to scoop up the food instead of a fork. If you fill them up, roll them, and fry them, you get flautas; if you bake or fry them flat, you get tostadas; cut them into triangles and fry them and you will get totopos (tortilla chips). Incredibly versatile, you can create multiple different dishes from just this one ingredient. Now you know why we all love tortillas.

Of course there is nothing like a freshly made tortilla, but there are plenty of good store-bought versions. Check around your city, particularly if you live in the Southwest U.S., and you might be surprised to find a *tortilleria* or a local Hispanic grocery store that sells them—it is here that you will get the best ones. When choosing store-bought tortillas, I recommend yellow corn as I often find the white corn packaged tortillas to have less taste. And read the ingredients—the less additives or preservatives, the better. There is an increasing variety available, including white, yellow, and blue corn; green tortillas made from the hoja santa herb (Mexican pepperleaf); or bright pink tortillas made by adding beetroot juice to the flour or corn dough before kneading.

FLOUR TORTILLAS

Flour tortillas are popular in northern Mexico and all over the border. They consist of three simple ingredients: flour, fat, and water. Many families have their own recipe and a dedicated person with the "special hand" in charge of making them. Some use butter, others lard and even olive oil. I've even made them with bacon fat. These subtle differences can make a magical tortilla recipe.

Flour tortillas are soft, fluffy, and pliable and can be stretched, stuffed, grilled, fried, or baked. Milder in flavor than corn tortillas, they are robust and can hold substantial fillings and take generous toppings.

CORN TORTILLAS

Like chiles, there are also over 50 types of corn, but heirloom corn is the key to making the best tortillas. Unfortunately this is not easily accessible, and it takes work to make a tortilla from scratch. Luckily there is masa harina, a processed corn flour that can be found in markets, grocery stores, or specialist Mexican shops if you want to make your own.

The richness and sweetness of corn makes these much more flavorful; they have more of a cornmeal texture, so are more grainy and also a lot more fragile. They aren't as "elastic" as flour tortillas, but they are matchless when fried: light and crunchy.

HEATING TORTILLAS

Tortillas can be toasted, fried, baked, or simply gently reheated to soften. Corn tortillas in particular can dry out quickly, as they have no gluten, but are easily softened again by reheating. Wrap them in a clean damp kitchen towel or tortilla warmer until you are ready to serve. If you don't have a warmer, place the towel-wrapped stack into a slightly larger bowl and cover it with a plate.

- Mist the tortilla with a little water before toasting on both sides in a pan, griddle, or comal for about 30 seconds per side. If the tortilla is fresh, it may briefly inflate.
- To microwave, place a tortilla on a plate and cover it with a damp paper towel. To reheat a stack, alternate tortillas with paper towels. Microwave on high for about 30 seconds. This method is best reserved for flour tortillas only.
- To reheat in the oven, preheat the oven to 250°F (120°C/ Gas mark ½). Place them in a casserole dish with a clean, damp kitchen towel and cover tightly with a lid or a piece of aluminum foil and heat for 15 to 20 minutes.

COOKING EQUIPMENT

You don't need any specialist equipment for the recipes in this book, other than a standard mortar and pestle and a blender or food processor. However, traditional equipment as listed here can often make all the difference to your experience of cooking as well as to the end result.

MOLCAJETE (MORTAR AND PESTLE): This Mexican version of a mortar and pestle is made of stone, traditionally carved out of a single block of vesicular basalt, round in shape with three legs. Used to grind ingredients, as well as prepare salsas and guacamole, it can withstand an open flame so can also be used for cooking or heating food.

TORTILLADORA (TORTILLA PRESS): If you are making your own tortillas, invest in one of these. It will help you create uniform, round, flat tortillas quickly and they will be exactly the correct thickness.

COMAL (GRIDDLE): A smooth flat griddle, predominantly used for cooking tortillas, searing meat, and toasting spices and nuts. See also page 45.

DISCO (DISCADA): Like a flattened wok, the traditional version was a steel farming plow disk used over an open flame. An ancient cooking technique, it enables you to cook large quantities of food and is associated with the dish *Discada* (see page 158). For those who like grilling food outdoors, this is a great option for barbecuing meats. It is sometimes referred to as a Mexican wok.

OLLA DE BARRO (CERAMIC BEAN POT): A lidded clay pot for cooking bean dishes, soups, or stews.

CAZUELA (CLAY DISH): Able to withstand high temperatures, this clay dish can go from stove-top to oven to table and is ideal for preparing rice and beans.

COOKING NOTES

When creating the recipes, please note the following.
- All tortillas used in the recipes throughout are 6 inches (15 cm) in diameter, except where noted for tostadas and burritos.
- Taco serving sizes are for the number of tacos made. Please allow 2 to 3 tacos per person—or more depending on appetite!
- Please follow either the US, Imperial, or metric measurements —don't swap them.

TACO-TASTIC TACOS!

The best tacos are your own inventions—the ones you create in your own kitchen with good ingredients and a dash of imagination! A little love and care taken will make every taco you make taste fantastic. Here are some tips on toppings, taco building, and taco eating.

TOPPINGS

Always start with the right foundation—a great tortilla—and then add your protein before carrying on with the toppings. Some of the suggestions here are not traditionally Mexican, but as I've said previously, you are your own master builder of tacos and anything goes. For taco parties, set out a range of different toppings so that people can pick and choose, and always have plenty of lime wedges available. Experiment and enjoy.

- Shredded iceberg lettuce or cabbage
- Crumbled cheese: cotija, queso, feta, Monterey Jack
- Sliced scallions (spring onion) and minced white onion
- Diced tomatoes or pico de gallo
- Sliced radish
- Pickled red onions or vegetables
- Salsas and aioli or mayonnaise
- Guacamole and sliced or chopped avocado
- Hot sauce
- Sliced fresh jalapeños
- Grilled vegetables
- Crema or sour cream
- Cilantro (coriander) leaves

TIPS FOR THE BEST TACOS

- Always use warm tortillas as they are soft, pliable, and will wrap around the ingredients without splitting.
- Add acid in the form of salsa, coleslaw, or lime juice.
- Pile on the pickles. Pickled onion and vegetables, jalapeños, cabbage—they all add unbeatable texture, flavor, and crunch.
- Choose the salsa to balance the taco dish—smoky flavors are the best all-rounders and avoid very hot or robust salsas for delicate dishes. If you are serving your salsa cold, make sure you add it as the last topping. If warm, try it under the protein.

- Taste your ingredients first; jalapeños you buy one day could be mild, but the next batch you buy could be a lot spicier.
- Understand your heat levels. If you are using a hot salsa or hot sauce, choose for flavor not heat. You should get a hit of heat that then fades away. Your mouth should not be burning for hours or you won't taste anything!
- Balance textures, such as something charred with something smooth, or something creamy with something crunchy. Meat tacos are great drizzled with something creamy on top such as crema or chopped avocado.
- Add color. Brightly colored chopped bell peppers, herb leaves, and picked red onion all add vibrancy.
- Mix it up so tastes intermingle. For example, if you have a tomato-based meat filling, don't add a tomato salsa as well.
- Consider the proportions of your ingredients and resist overfilling the taco. You want to get a taste of all the different elements in each bite.

1

Salsas

Playing a huge role in Mexican food is the endlessly versatile salsa. The classic red salsa, with its kick of chile, and green tomatillo salsa are staples every taco fan should know how to make, but here are recipes for other condiments that add their own unique flavorings too, from the fiery salsa macha to the mild avocado crema.

There are so many interesting ways to enjoy salsas. Use them as dips, toppings, and marinades, or spoon them into soups and stews. They can dress salads, or be eaten as a relish with grilled fish or meat.

SALSA ROJA DE MESA

HOMEMADE RED SALSA

MAKES 2 CUPS

Chiles de árbol provide a real kick of heat, being up to six times hotter than the typical jalapeño pepper. They have a smoky, nutty, and grassy flavor profile that is perfect for this robust salsa. Serve the salsa with grilled meats or eggs, or use it for dipping with totopos (tortilla chips).

4 cloves garlic, peeled
¼ cup (2 fl oz/60 ml) olive oil
4 large tomatoes, halved
½ large white onion, quartered
2 oz (55 g) dried chiles de árbol or Thai (bird's eye) chiles, stems removed
1 teaspoon dried oregano
Sea salt, to taste

Preheat the oven to 400°F (200°C/Gas mark 6).

Wrap the garlic cloves in aluminum foil with 1 teaspoon of the oil and place in a baking pan with the remaining oil, tomatoes, and onion. Bake in the oven for 10 to 15 minutes. Five minutes before the end of the cooking time, remove the pan and add the chiles de árbol or Thai (bird's eye) chiles. Return to the oven. When the tomatoes and onions are charred and the chiles turn a little darker, remove from the oven.

Take the garlic out of the foil and add all the ingredients, with oregano and salt, to a blender or food processor. Process to your desired consistency—briefly for a chunky style or longer for a smooth result. Taste and adjust the seasoning, if necessary. Serve immediately or store, covered, in a refrigerator for 3 to 5 days.

SALSA VERDE DE MESA
HOMEMADE ROASTED TOMATILLO SALSA

MAKES 3 CUPS

The tomatillo is a favorite ingredient in Mexico, where this native green tomato is often added to dishes for its fresh tangy, citrus flavor. The firm, green fruit makes a tangy, light salsa, ideal for serving with poultry or fish or for dipping with totopos (tortilla chips). The sugar in the recipe helps balance the acidity from the tomatillos.

10 small tomatillos, cut in half if large, husks removed, and rinsed well
1 large white onion, quartered
5 large jalapeño chiles, stems removed (and seeded, if you want to reduce the heat)
5 cloves garlic, peeled
3 tablespoons vegetable oil
½ bunch fresh cilantro (coriander) with stems, coarsely chopped
1 teaspoon sugar
Sea salt and freshly ground black pepper, to taste

Preheat the broiler (grill) to high heat.

In a large baking pan, spread out an even layer of the tomatillos, onion, jalapeños, and garlic. Drizzle the oil over the vegetables, making sure they are evenly coated. Broil for 10 to 15 minutes, checking them halfway through the cooking time. They should be a little charred but not burned. When they begin to turn dark, remove them and let cool.

Transfer the vegetables to a blender or food processor (be sure to include the drippings). Add the cilantro and sugar, then season with salt and black pepper. Pulse blend at 5-second intervals until you have a chunky consistency. Taste and adjust the seasoning, if necessary. Serve immediately or store, covered, in a refrigerator for 3 to 5 days.

Fresh tomatillos are the best choice for this recipe, but if you can't find them, substitute canned tomatillos. Alternatively, try replacing them with cape gooseberries (also called ground cherries or physalis) or under-ripe green cherry tomatoes along with a tablespoon of lime or lemon juice. You'll have a perfectly fine salsa, although the taste will not be exactly the same as one made with fresh tomatillos.

SALSA TAQUERA
STREET TACO SALSA

MAKES 3 CUPS

Here is a salsa made from *calabacita*, meaning "little squash" in Spanish. A type of summer squash, there are two types popular in Mexico: *calabacita larga*, or "long little squash," and *calabacita bola*, or "round little squash." You can use zucchini (courgette) or a similar type of summer (soft-rind) squash as a substitute. Serve this tasty green salsa with tacos, pasta, grilled meats, and more.

1 cup (8 fl oz/240 ml) avocado oil, grapeseed oil, or olive oil
6 jalapeño chiles, sliced in quarters lengthwise (membrane removed and seeded, if you want to reduce to heat)
½ onion, sliced
2 medium calabacita or zucchini (courgette), sliced into ½-inch (12-mm) rounds
6 cloves garlic, peeled
½ cup (4 fl oz/120 ml) water
Sea salt and freshly ground black pepper, to taste

Place a large sauté pan over a medium-high heat and add half the oil. When it is hot, add the jalapeños, onion, calabacita, and garlic. Sauté for about 5 minutes, until all vegetables are soft, then add a few splashes of the water to prevent the vegetables from browning. Remove, place in a container, and let cool.

Put all vegetables into a blender, cover, and remove the small middle cap. Season with salt and pepper and blend at medium-high speed. When it is smooth, reduce the speed to medium-low and gradually start adding the remaining oil in a thin stream until the salsa has reached a smooth and creamy consistency.

Taste and adjust the seasoning, if necessary. If the salsa separates, remedy it by adding water by the tablespoon. Serve immediately or store, covered, in the refrigerator for 3 to 5 days.

SALSA MOLCAJETEADA
STONE MORTAR SALSA

MAKES 2–3 CUPS

Traditionally, this salsa is made over a charcoal or wood fire, which adds an unbelievably delicious, smoky flavor. The next time you have a BBQ, after you've finished grilling, make this salsa—simply toss the ingredients on your grill rack and let the smoke do its magic. You can make this salsa indoors, but it may not have the same flavor.

2 tomatoes
4 large jalapeño chiles
½ white onion
4 cloves garlic, peeled
Sea salt and freshly ground black
    pepper, to taste

Put a comal or flat griddle (grill) pan over a high heat. When it is hot, add the whole tomatoes, whole jalapeño chiles, onion, and garlic to the dry pan (no fat is added).

When the vegetables begin to char after about 2 to 5 minutes, turn them over to char the other side for the same amount of time, until charred on both sides. Remove each ingredient as it is ready—the garlic cloves are usually the first ones to be removed from the pan.

Coarsely chop the vegetables and put all the ingredients into a molcajete (see below) and pound them with the pestle until you have a chunky consistency. Season with salt and black pepper.

If you don't have a molcajete, a Mexican-style mortar and pestle made from stone, you can use a blender or food processor on the pulse setting. However, using a mortar and pestle will help release the oils, adding more flavors to the salsa.

MORITA AIOLI

MORITA MAYONNAISE

MAKES 2 CUPS

This creamy, smoky aioli (a kind of garlicky mayonnaise) goes well
with seafood tacos. This version is made with morita chiles, which
are dried and smoked and are a more fiery version of chipotles.
Try to find the purée or paste form, which will permeate the dish;
otherwise you can use finely chopped chiles as a substitute.

2 egg yolks
4 cloves garlic, peeled and grated
1½ teaspoons lemon juice or distilled
   white vinegar
1 tablespoon chipotle or morita purée
   or paste
½ teaspoon ground black pepper
½ teaspoon sea salt
1 cup (8 fl oz/240 ml) avocado oil (you
   can substitute grapeseed or olive oil)

Add the egg yolks, garlic, lemon juice, morita purée, black
pepper, and salt to a blender or food processor.

With the blender running at a medium speed, slowly start adding
the oil in a thin stream. To prevent the emulsion from breaking
up, do not let the blender or processor get too hot, which can
happen by operating it at too high a speed or for too long a period
of time. If it is too thick, add a tablespoon of water to help the
emulsification process.

When smooth, serve immediately or store, covered, in the
refrigerator for 2 to 3 days.

CREMA DE AGUACATE

AVOCADO CREMA

MAKES 3 CUPS

Avocados have played an important role in the Mexican diet for thousands of years—at least 10,000 years ago, based on evidence found by archaeologists in Central Mexico—and it is thought avocado trees were first cultivated about 5,000 years ago. This recipe for avocado crema makes a great topping for all kinds of tacos, adding a vibrant yet creamy touch.

2 small or 1 large avocado
1 jalapeño chile
1 cup (8½ oz/240 g) sour cream or
 Greek-style plain (natural) yogurt
⅓ cup (3 fl oz/90 ml) milk
6 sprigs fresh cilantro (coriander)
Juice of 1 lime
½ teaspoon ground black pepper
½ teaspoon garlic powder
Sea salt, to taste

Halve and pit (stone) the avocado and scoop the flesh into a blender or food processor.

Coarsely chop the jalapeño and add to the blender along with the remaining ingredients.

Blend until smooth and adjust the seasoning to taste, if necessary. Serve immediately or store, covered, in the refrigerator for 3 to 5 days.

SALSA MACHA

MEXICAN CHILE OIL

MAKES 2 CUPS

Made with dried chiles, nuts, and oil, this salsa has crispy pieces that add crunch, a little like an Asian chile oil. It hails from Veracruz, but there are other versions depending on the region. Peanuts, for example, are traditionally used in this slightly spicy, nutty, tangy salsa, but some recipes use different nuts. Spoon it over your favorite Mexican dishes, such as tacos or quesadillas.

6 dried chiles de árbol
4 dried ancho chiles
2 cups (16 fl oz/475 ml) avocado oil
6 cloves garlic, peeled and minced
¼ cup (1¼ oz/35 g) crushed peanuts
2 tablespoons sesame seeds
Raisins (optional)
Sea salt, to taste

Remove the stems and seeds from the chiles, then chop them into small pieces.

Put a wide skillet or frying pan over a medium-high heat and add the oil. When the oil is hot, carefully add the chiles, garlic, peanuts, and sesame seeds. Cook for about 5 minutes, until the garlic starts to crisp and the seeds turn golden. Remove from the heat, stir in the raisins, if using, and let cool. Season to taste.

Serve immediately or store in an airtight container or jar for up to a month.

Overleaf, page 35, clockwise:
Morita Mayonnaise, Mexican Chile Oil,
Avocado Crema, Stone Mortar Salsa.

SALSA CRUDA DE SERRANO CON PEPINO
SERRANO-CUCUMBER SALSA

MAKES 6 CUPS

Here is a rustic salsa that provides the perfect balance between the coolness of cucumber, the tart, slightly citrusy flavor of the popular Mexican tomatillo, and the heat of serrano chile. Serrano chiles—the second most popular chile in Mexico—are named after the mountain ridges on which they grow. This salsa is delicious served alongside salmon or another fish, but if you prefer, use it as a dip for totopos (tortilla chips).

2 cups (7 oz/200 g) chopped cucumber
½ cup (2½ oz/75 g) chopped serrano chiles
1 cup (4½ oz/125 g) chopped tomatillos
1 cup (2 oz/60 g) chopped scallions (spring onions)
¼ cup (1¼ oz/35 g) chopped garlic
½ cup (¾ oz/20 g) chopped fresh cilantro (coriander)
¼ cup (2 fl oz/60 ml) lime juice
1 cup (5¼ oz/150 g) cubed avocado
Sea salt and freshly ground black pepper, to taste

In a food processor or blender, add all ingredients except for the avocado and pulse until you have a chunky consistency.

Transfer the salsa to a bowl and fold in the avocado cubes. Taste and adjust the seasoning, if needed. Serve immediately or store, covered, in the refrigerator for 3 to 5 days.

PICO DE GALLO CON PIÑA ASADA
PINEAPPLE PICO DE GALLO

MAKES 6 CUPS

A pico de gallo is made with freshly chopped ingredients. It is similar to a salsa but has less liquid. This version includes pineapple, giving it a bright, citrusy, sweet flavor that is great with seafood. Broiling or grilling the pineapple first is not essential but the method will caramelize its sugars and enhance the sweetness.

¼ pineapple
3 large tomatoes
¼ large red onion
2 jalapeño chiles
8 stems fresh cilantro (coriander), minced
Juice of 2 limes
1 tablespoon olive oil
1 teaspoon ground black pepper
Sea salt, to taste

Using a sharp knife, slice off the pineapple rind, cut away and discard the tough core, and slice the flesh into ¼-inch (6-mm)-thick pieces. If you want, grill the pineapple pieces on a barbecue or in a ridged grill (griddle) pan over medium heat for 2 to 3 minutes per side, until you see dark grill marks, and let cool.

Dice the grilled pineapple into small pieces and transfer to a medium mixing bowl. Dice the tomatoes, red onion and jalapeños, and add them to the mixing bowl along with the fresh cilantro. Mix to combine.

Squeeze the juice of the 2 limes into the bowl, then add the olive oil, black pepper, and salt. Mix, taste, and adjust the seasoning, if necessary. It can be made spicier by adding more jalapeño chiles, sweeter by adding more pineapple, or, if you love acidity, add more lime juice.

Serve immediately or store, covered, in the refrigerator for 3 to 5 days.

Pico de gallo, meaning "rooster's beak," is also called salsa cruda. To make regular pico de gallo, simply omit the pineapple in the recipe.

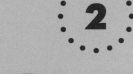

2

Tortillas and Sides

Great tacos begins with the tortilla, and here you will find easy recipes to make your own flour and corn varieties. That might seem like a big effort, especially when you can buy store-bought versions so easily, but homemade tortillas really make the meal.

Included here are some sides that will add to your taco experience, from blistering pan-fried chiles to refried beans, pickled vegetables and onions to pile on top of tacos, and, of course, homemade tortilla chips, or totopos, which are a great way to make use of stale tortillas.

TORTILLAS DE HARINA DE MAMA

MOM'S FLOUR TORTILLAS

MAKES 12

One of the most comforting things that I can remember as a child is the smell of buttery tortillas made by my grandmother. A good flour tortilla should be soft and not too thick, and making your own is the best way to enjoy them—you probably already have all the ingredients and equipment you'll need in your own kitchen.

. . . .

2 cups (8¾ oz/250 g) all-purpose (plain) flour, plus extra flour for dusting

1 teaspoon baking powder

1½ teaspoons salt

1 cup (8 fl oz/240 ml) whole (full-fat) milk, warmed

5 tablespoons (2½ oz/70 g) unsalted butter, melted

In a mixing bowl, mix the flour with the baking powder and salt. Form a hole in the middle of the dry ingredients. Gradually add the warm milk and melted butter, using a plastic spatula (palette knife) to combine the ingredients well until you have a smooth dough.

Shape the dough into a ball, cover with a damp cloth or plastic wrap (clingfilm), and let rest for 20 minutes. This step is important for letting the gluten relax, which will make the tortilla rolling process easier.

Clean and lightly dust a flat work surface with flour. Transfer the dough to the work surface and start forming 2-oz (55-g) balls about the size of a lemon. Dust the surface again, if needed, and dust a rolling pin with flour, then start rolling out the balls into 6-inch (15-cm)-diameter tortillas. The dough should look translucent when you hold a tortilla up to the light (a thick tortilla will be too stiff). Stack the tortillas with sheets of parchment (baking) paper between them so they don't stick together.

Put a nonstick comal or flat griddle (grill) pan over high heat, and when it is hot, reduce the heat to medium-high—you want the heat to be high enough to create some dark marks. One at a time, cook each tortilla for 20 seconds on one side, then turn it over and cook for an additional 5 seconds.

Derived from the Aztec Nahuatl word *comalli*, the comal is a traditional Mexican flat griddle, available in clay, cast iron, stainless steel, or aluminum. Endlessly versatile, not only is it excellent for cooking or reheating tortillas, it can be used to sear meat, toast spices, sauté vegetables, grill fish, or fry potatoes.

TORTILLAS DE MAÍZ
CORN TORTILLAS

MAKES 12

To make authentic Mexican corn tortillas, you'll need to use masa harina, a traditional Mexican corn flour that is made by soaking cooked corn kernels in lime before they are ground. Masa harina gives the tortillas—as well as tamales and tostadas—a light, tangy taste. And better yet, because it is gluten free, these tortillas are suitable for people with a gluten intolerance.

2 cups (8½ oz/240 g) masa harina
1 teaspoon of salt
1½ cups (12 fl oz/350 ml) warm water
(you may need more or less)

In a mixing bowl, mix the masa harina with the salt, then gradually start adding the water until you have a smooth but moist dough. It is ready when you can easy form a small ball and press your index finger into it without the dough cracking too much or the dough sticking to your hands. Cover the dough with a damp cloth or plastic wrap (clingfilm).

Put a nonstick comal or flat griddle (grill) pan over a high heat, and when it is hot, reduce the heat to medium-high—you want the heat to be high enough to create some dark marks. If the pan is not hot enough, the tortillas will stick.

Make the tortillas one at a time. For each tortilla, roll a 2-oz (55-g) ball of dough, the size of a lemon, in your hands. To shape, press it between two square sheets of parchment (baking paper) until flat and 6 inches (15 cm) in diameter, or use a tortilla press (see the box opposite), applying enough pressure to make it thin.

Place the tortilla in the pan and let cook for 25 seconds without moving it. Turn it over and cook the other side for 10 to 15 seconds, until the tortilla turns opaque, then turn it over again and cook for an additional 5 to 10 seconds.

If you want to eat the tortillas immediately, keep your tortillas warm under a clean kitchen towel. If not, let them cool and store in a sealed bag for up to 3 days. If they start to get dry, you can turn them into tortilla chips (see page 50).

The best way to shape tortillas is with a tortilla press, but if you don't have one, simply use a heavy, flat object to help you press the dough balls. You'll need two square sheets of parchment (baking) paper to protect the surfaces from the sticky dough. Place one square on the bottom of the press or on the work surface, place a masa ball in the center, then top with the remaining square. Lower the lid of the press, or place a heavy, flat object on top, and press down. To transfer the tortilla to the pan, lift off the top sheet, flip the tortilla side into your hand, remove the square that's now on top, and carefully slide the tortilla into the pan.

TOTOPOS ENCHILADOS

SEASONED TORTILLA CHIPS

SERVES 6

Totopos are a must-have at any party! Although they are the perfect vehicle for your favorite dips and salsas, these delicious chips have enough flavor to be tasty on their own. For the best authentic tortilla chips, follow the Corn Tortillas recipe (see page 46) to make your own tortillas. If you're short of time, you can use the store-bought variety.

12 corn tortillas, cut into triangles (pie style)
8 cups (3½ pints/2 liters) peanut (groundnut) oil

Seasoning
4 tablespoons salt
2 tablespoons sugar
1 tablespoon onion powder
1 tablespoon guajillo or paprika chile powder
1 tablespoon chipotle or chile powder

In a mixing bowl, add all the seasoning ingredients and mix together. Transfer to a sugar shaker, lidded glass jar, or other container.

Heat the oil in a deep pot placed over a high heat until a cooking thermometer reaches 350°F (180°C).

Carefully lower a batch of tortilla triangles into the oil, making sure you don't add too many to avoid reducing the temperature of the oil. When the color changes to a golden light brown, remove the tortilla chips with a spider or skimming spoon and place them on a baking sheet. Sprinkle the seasoning evenly across the tortilla chips as soon are you lay them on the sheet—if you wait too long, the seasoning will not stick to them.

Let cool and store in an airtight container or resealable bag.

To cook crispy totopos without burning them, use a thermometer to keep the oil temperature steady. If you don't have a cooking thermometer, here's how to tell if the oil is at the right temperature. Drop one of the tortilla triangles into the oil: If there are no bubbles or a few air bubbles that are moving slowly, your oil is not hot enough. If there is smoke coming out of the oil and the tortilla turns dark within 30 seconds, your oil is too hot.

CHILES TOREADOS
MEXICAN BLISTERED CHILES

SERVES 4

This popular dish is traditionally served hot or at room temperature in *taquerias* **(a Mexican restaurant that specializes in tacos) for topping tacos, grilled meats, and other dishes. It adds a bomb of smoky, spicy, and acidic flavor. You can also cook these blistered chiles over an outdoor barbecue grill.**

4 whole jalapeño chiles, shishito chiles, or Padrón peppers
¼ yellow (brown) onion
2 tablespoons avocado oil
1 tablespoon salsa inglesa, Worcestershire sauce, or soy sauce
Juice of 1 lime
Sea salt, to taste
Black and white sesame seeds, to garnish

Leaving the stems on, quarter the jalapeño chiles lengthwise; if they are small, slice them in half. Slice the yellow (brown) onion into thin strips.

Heat the oil in a sauté pan over a high heat. Be careful not to burn the oil—it should be hot but not smoking. Add the jalapeños in a single layer and let them sit. Do not stir.

When the chiles start to turn brown, turn them over and cook the other side. Remove when they are charred and blistered on both sides and transfer to a serving dish.

Immediately add the onion to the pan and sauté for 3 to 5 minutes, until they caramelize.

Remove the onion and add to the dish with the jalapeños. Squeeze in the lime juice, add the Worcestershire or soy sauce, sprinkle with sesame seeds if using, and season with salt to taste. Serve warm.

Chiles toreados can be prepared up to a week ahead and stored in an airtight container in the refrigerator. When you are ready to serve them, reheat the chiles gently by sautéing in a little vegetable oil or let them come to room temperature before serving.

GUACAMOLE

GUACAMOLE

MAKES 3 CUPS

A dish made by the Aztecs in South Central Mexico prior to the sixteenth century, guacamole did not become well-known in the United States until the mid-twentieth century, partly due to bans on Mexican avocado imports. The modern name derives from the Nahuatl word, *āhuacamōlli,* which literally translates as "avocado sauce." There are many versions of guacamole, all of which should deliver a creamy, acidic, and spicy accompaniment.

1 small roma (plum) tomato
¼ red onion
1 large jalapeño chile
4 sprigs fresh cilantro (coriander)
4 medium avocados
2 tablespoons lime juice
1 teaspoon cracked black peppercorns
Sea salt, to taste
1 tablespoon avocado or olive oil
  (optional)
Pico de gallo (see box page 38),
  to serve

Coarsely chop the tomato, onion, and jalapeño. Chop the fresh cilantro, making sure to include some of the stem. Add the vegetables and herb to a medium mixing bowl.

Halve and pit (stone) the avocados, then scoop the flesh into the mixing bowl. Add the lime juice, season with salt and black pepper, and combine. Taste and adjust the seasoning, if necessary. Top with pico de gallo, if desired.

If you want to store your guacamole in the refrigerator for a couple of days, mix in the avocado or olive oil to prevent oxidation.

CEBOLLA ROJA EN ESCABECHE
PICKLED RED ONIONS

MAKES 3 CUPS

Onions marinated with habanero chile are a popular accompaniment in the Mexican state of Yucatán, and versions made with white onions are common in other Mexican states. These pickled onions are pungent, crisp, and colorful—perfect for adding some zing to your favorite dishes. When cutting the onions, make the slices thick enough to add some crunch.

3 large red onions
1 red or orange fresh habanero chile
1 teaspoon whole black peppercorns
1 teaspoon dried cilantro (coriander)
1 sprig thyme
2 bay leaves
1 tablespoon sugar
1 tablespoon salt
2 cups (16 fl oz/475 ml) apple cider vinegar or distilled white vinegar
1 cup (8 fl oz/240 ml) water

Cut the red onions into thin slices. Cut the habanero into thin slices, removing the membrane and seeds if you prefer less heat. Peel the carrot and cut it into thin rounds.

Place the onions and carrot into a large 32-oz (1-liter) glass preserving jar (or two smaller jars). Make sure you leave enough room for the pickling liquid.

In a small saucepan, add the spices, herbs, sugar, and salt along with the vinegar and water. Bring to a boil over a medium heat, stir, and then carefully pour over the vegetables in the jar. Let cool, then seal the lid. The pickled red onions will keep in the refrigerator for up to 4 weeks.

VEGETALES EN ESCABECHE
PICKLED VEGETABLES

MAKES 4 CUPS

These crunchy Mexican pickled vegetables are great toppings for tacos, delivering piquancy and zesty brightness, and can be included with salads, sandwiches, or eggs. They also make a tasty appetizer alongside chips and salsa. Experiment with your own favorite additions, such as garlic cloves, sliced radish, bell pepper, or beets.

- -

1 red onion
1 large carrot
3 jalapeño chiles
2 cups small cauliflower florets
½ tablespoon whole black peppercorns
½ tablespoon dried cilantro (coriander)
2 bay leaves
1 tablespoon salt
1 tablespoon sugar
2 cups (16 fl oz/475 ml) apple cider
  vinegar or distilled white vinegar
1 cup (8 fl oz/240 ml) water

Cut the red onion into thin slices. Peel the carrot and cut it into ¼-inch (6-mm)-thick rounds. Cut the chiles into ½-inch (12-mm)-thick slices.

Place the onion, carrot, jalapeños, and cauliflower in a large 32-oz (1-liter) glass preserving jar (or two smaller jars). Make sure you leave enough room for the pickling liquid.

Add spices, herbs, salt, sugar, vinegar, and water to a saucepan. Bring to a boil, then immediately turn off the heat to prevent evaporation. While the pickling liquid is still hot, carefully pour into the jar until the liquid has covered all the vegetables. Seal and place in the fridge; it is best to leave them overnight before consuming. The vegetables will keep in the refrigerator for up to 4 weeks.

FRIJOLES NEGROS REFRITOS
REFRIED BLACK BEANS

MAKES 2½ CUPS

The English translation for *frijoles refritos*, "refried beans," is misleading, because while the beans are cooked twice, they aren't fried twice! The beans are first boiled and mashed, and then cooked a second time by frying in oil. Refried beans can be made with pinto or red kidney beans, but this recipe uses dried black beans. They can be served alongside most mains, whether based on meat, chicken, fish, seafood, eggs, or vegetarian.

1¼ cups (8 oz/225 g) dried black beans
½ small white onion, peeled and trimmed
1 jalapeño chile
3 cloves garlic, peeled
2 bay leaves
1 tablespoon salt
2 tablespoons vegetable oil
Sea salt and freshly ground black pepper, to taste
Sliced jalapeños and cubed queso fresco or feta cheese, to garnish

Sort through the beans and rinse in cold water. Add the beans to a pot, cover with water, and bring to a boil.

When the water is boiling, add the onion, jalapeño, garlic, bay leaves, and salt. Cover and let simmer for 40 minutes. Be sure to keep an eye on the pot so that it always has enough water. Add more water if the beans start to become dry.

To test if the beans are ready, scoop a couple out and press on them with your fingers or a spoon. They should be soft. If not, cook for an additional 5 minutes and test again.

When the beans are cooked, use a ladle to scoop all the ingredients, except the bay leaves (remove and discard them), into mixing bowl and hand-mash them. Alternatively, scoop into a blender and blend until smooth.

Bring a large sauté pan to a medium-high heat and add the oil. When hot, add the bean mixture—be careful, because it will bubble and splatter. Stir continuously with a spatula or wooden spoon until the beans are no longer runny and have a thicker consistency. Taste and adjust the seasoning, if necessary, and garnish with jalapeños and cheese to serve.

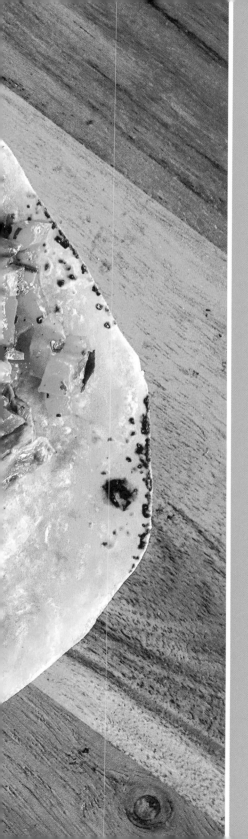

Breakfast Tacos

Eggs make the perfect ingredient for a morning taco, as they taste amazing when layered with salsas and cheese. Although you are probably familiar with huevos rancheros, there are many other ways to eat a Mexican breakfast, and here are recipes for huevos de granja and huevos verdes.

Migas—tortillas and scrambled eggs—might be new to you but they are a family favorite. And we couldn't talk about the first meal of the day without offering a burrito recipe, which can be served as a taco if you prefer.

HUEVOS VERDES
GREEN EGGS

MAKES 10

Here is a variation of a popular dish enjoyed in Mexican farms at breakfast time: *huevos rancheros*, or ranch eggs, which are fried eggs served in corn tortillas. Instead of fried eggs, however, we've pimped them up by cooking the eggs like you would for a frittata and adding refreshing green vegetables and seasonings.

6 eggs
½ cup (½ oz/15 g) spinach
2 fresh tomatillos, husked and chopped
1 scallion (spring onion), chopped
2 jalapeño chiles, chopped
2 fresh cilantro (coriander) sprigs, chopped
1 tablespoon vegetable oil
10 corn tortillas
Sea salt and freshly ground black pepper, to taste

Toppings
Chopped avocado
Mexican Chile Oil (see page 33)

In a mixing bowl, add the eggs, season with salt and pepper, and whisk well.

Add the spinach, tomatillos, scallion, jalapeños, and cilantro to a blender or food processor. Season with salt and pepper and blend until you have a lightly chunky texture.

Heat the oil in a nonstick skillet or frying pan over medium heat, then add the spinach mixture. Let simmer for 5 minutes, then add the egg mixture. Fold in until the eggs are cooked.

Briefly heat the tortillas on a comal or flat griddle (grill) pan to warm them, then fill with the cooked eggs and enjoy as is or add the toppings!

When whisking the eggs, make sure you whisk them vigorously, which will create air bubbles that will result in fluffier eggs!

HUEVOS DE GRANJA
FARM-STYLE EGGS

MAKES 6

Before the arrival of the Spaniards, and with them chickens, people in Mexico enjoyed eggs from local sources, such as turkey, muscovy duck, quail, pheasant, and insects. Today, Mexico is in one of the world's top chicken egg producers, and eggs are enjoyed in numerous Mexican dishes from soup to desserts, and, of course, for breakfast.

2 tablespoons (1 oz/30 g) butter
1 tablespoon minced yellow (brown) or white onion
1 tablespoon minced garlic
¼ cup (1 oz/30 g) chopped yellow, orange, or red bell pepper
¼ cup (1 oz/30 g) chopped calabacitas or zucchini (courgette)
½ cup (2½ oz/75 g) halved cherry tomatoes
¼ cup (¾ oz/20 g) sliced white button mushrooms
2 tablespoons cooked yellow corn kernels
4 eggs, beaten
1 cup (1 oz/30 g) torn spinach
6 corn or flour tortillas
Refried Black Beans (see page 60), topped with crumbled queso fresco or cotija cheese, to serve
Homemade Roasted Tomatillo Salsa (optional; see page 27)

Melt the butter in a wide lidded skillet or frying pan over a medium heat. Add the onions, garlic, and bell peppers and cook for a few minutes until the onion is translucent.

Add the calabacitas or zucchini, cover with a lid, and cook for 3 minutes. When the calabacitas begins to soften, add the cherry tomatoes, mushrooms, and corn, and cook without the lid, stirring occasionally, for 3 minutes more.

Pour in the eggs and cook for a few minutes until the eggs have almost set but are still a little runny, then fold in the spinach.

Briefly heat the tortillas on a comal or flat griddle (grill) pan to warm them, then fill with the cooked eggs. Serve with cooked black beans and the tomatillo salsa, if using.

FRIJOLES CON CHORIZO Y QUESO

BEANS, CHORIZO, AND CHEESE BURRITO

MAKES 6

Basically fried pork belly or rind, chicharrones are found throughout Spain and Latin America. In Mexico, they can be the main ingredient in a dish served with a salsa and they are also found in supermarkets as finger-food snacks. In this recipe, a larger tortilla has been used and rolled up burrito style, but you can also serve the filling in 6-inch (15-cm) tacos.

1 tablespoon vegetable oil
½ cup (2½ oz/70 g) diced chorizo
1 tablespoon minced onion
1 cup (8½ oz/240 g) Refried Black Beans (see page 60)
Sea salt and freshly ground black pepper, to taste
¼ cup (1 oz/30 g) shredded quesillo cheese, mozzarella, or Monterey Jack
6 flour tortillas, 12-inch (30-cm) in diameter

Toppings
2 tablespoons chicharrones, fried pork rind, or crispy bacon pieces
Chopped fresh cilantro (coriander)
Mexican crema or sour cream

Heat the vegetable oil in a skillet or frying pan over a medium-high heat and add the chorizo. When the fat starts to melt, add the onion. When the onion is translucent, add in the black beans, then mix it all together in the pan until the beans start to simmer. Taste and adjust seasoning if necessary.

Add the shredded cheese on top of the bean mixture, cover, and heat until the cheese has melted.

Briefly heat the tortillas on a comal or flat griddle (grill) pan to warm them, then divide the bean mixture among the tortillas and top with the crispy chicharrones and the cilantro. Fold each tortilla burrito-style by folding in the sides first and rolling the tortilla up from the bottom. Cut each burrito in half. Drizzle over crema or sour cream to serve.

> Quesillo cheese, also called Oaxaca cheese because it originated in the Mexican state of Oaxaca, is a type of fresh cow's milk cheese with a tangy flavor. This stringy, stretchy cheese is ideal for melting. If you can't find it in your grocery store, use Monterey Jack cheese or mozzarella cheese as a substitute.

PAPAS A LA MEXICANA CON PANCETTA

MEXICAN POTATOES AND PANCETTA

MAKES 4

Potatoes may have been growing wild in Mexico before the arrival of the Spaniards in the sixteenth century, but it was the Spaniards who introduced the cultivated plant to the country, and since then it has become a staple food. The Mexican name for potato, *papas,* is from the Quechua language of the Incas.

6 oz (175 g) pancetta or thick
   bacon, chopped
½ cup (2½ oz/75 g) diced potatoes
2 teaspoons vegetable oil
¼ cup (1½ oz/45 g) diced tomato
2 tablespoons minced onion
2 tablespoons minced jalapeño chile
2 eggs, beaten
Sea salt and freshly ground black
   pepper, to taste
4 flour tortillas

Toppings
Sliced scallions (spring onions)
Shredded quesillo cheese, Monterey
   Jack, or mozzarella (optional)

Put a nonstick or cast-iron skillet or frying pan over a medium-high heat. When hot, add the pancetta and sauté until most of the fat melts and the pancetta starts to get crispy. Transfer the pancetta to a bowl.

Add the potatoes to the skillet and add a little vegetable oil, if necessary. Sauté and cover for 6 to 8 minutes. When the potatoes are almost cooked, add the tomato, onion, and jalapeños. Sauté until the onion is translucent.

In a mixing bowl, add the eggs, season with salt and pepper, and whisk vigorously. Pour the eggs into the skillet and stir until cooked.

Briefly heat the tortillas on a comal or flat griddle (grill) pan to warm them, then divide the potato mixture among the tortillas and top with the crispy pancetta as well as the avocado slices and shredded cheese.

BISTEC A LA MEXICANA

STEAK AND EGGS, MEXICAN STYLE

MAKES 6

If *bistec* sounds familiar, it might be because it is derived from the English "beef steak." The salsa for this hearty dish is made with ingredients that represent the colors of the Mexican national flag: white onion, red tomato, and green chile.

1 rib-eye steak, at room temperature
Vegetable oil, for brushing
2 tablespoons (1 oz/30 g) butter
¼ cup (1¼ oz/35 g) chopped
   white onion
1 tablespoon minced garlic
¼ cup (1 oz/25 g) ¼-inch (6-mm)-thick
   sliced jalapeño chiles
½ cup (3 oz/85 g) diced tomato
6 eggs
6 corn or flour tortillas
Sea salt and freshly ground black
   pepper, to taste

Heat a cast-iron skillet or frying pan over a medium-high heat. Rub both sides of the steak with oil. Season with salt and pepper.

Put the steak into the skillet—you should hear a nice sizzle. Cook for about 2 to 3 minutes until the bottom side of the steak has a golden crust. Turn it over and cook for an additional 2 to 3 minutes.

When both sides are seared, reduce the heat to medium, drop the butter into the pan, and tilt it toward you to scoop up the melted butter with a spoon and baste the top of the steak for 2 minutes on each side. Remove the steak from the skillet and let rest on a cutting (chopping) board for 10 minutes.

In the same skillet, add the onion, garlic, and jalapeño, then cook, stirring occasionally, until the onion is translucent. Add the tomatoes, then turn off the heat.

In a separate nonstick skillet or frying pan over a medium-low heat, cook the eggs sunny-side-up (without turning them over).

Meanwhile, slice the steak into ½-inch (12-mm)-thick strips.

Briefly heat the tortillas on a comal or flat griddle (grill) pan to warm them, then layer the steak on the bottom, a fried egg on top, and finish with the cooked tomato salsa. Season to taste.

MIGAS
CRISPY TORTILLA AND EGGS

MAKES 6

Migas are one my favorite childhood dishes. A simple and comforting dish, it is a common saying in Mexico that when someone has cooked *migas* for you, it is because they love you. Although this recipe is technically not a taco, it is made with tortillas and delicious for breakfast. You can also use it as a taco filling, too.

2 tablespoons vegetable oil
4 tortillas, cut into 6 triangles (pie style)
1 tablespoon minced onion
4 eggs, beaten
Sea salt and freshly ground black pepper, to taste

Toppings
Shredded quesillo cheese, Monterey Jack, or mozzarella
1 cup (8½ oz/240 g) Refried Black Beans, warmed (see page 60)
Stone Mortar Salsa (optional; see page 30)

Heat the oil in a skillet or frying pan over a medium-high heat. When it is hot, add the tortilla triangles and cook for about 2 minutes, until they are crispy, then turn over and cook for an additional 2 minutes, until crispy on both sides.

Reduce the heat to medium, add the minced onion, and cook for a few minutes until the onion is translucent.

Meanwhile, beat the eggs in a bowl and season with salt and pepper. Add the eggs to the skillet and stir until the eggs are cooked.

Turn the heat off, then serve the eggs topped with the shredded cheese and accompanied by refried black beans and salsa.

4

Meat and Poultry

Many of Mexico's well-loved dishes feature pork, beef, or chicken (or combinations of all three) as the main ingredient, and that applies to tacos, too.

From grilled skewers to slow-roasted pulled pork and beef to filling stews, crispy carnitas, and spicy chorizo, there's a taco for every meat lover in this chapter. Here is where rich marinades, purées, chiles, citrus, herbs, and spices can really impart their delicious flavors to fullest effect in such traditional dishes as the pibil, tinga, and picadillo.

PUERCO EN SALSA VERDE

GREEN CHILE PORK STEW

MAKES 10

There are several variations on the Mexican name for this *guisado*, or stew, including *chile verde con cerdo*, *cerdo en salsa verde*, and *carne de puerco en salsa verde*, but there are even more variations on the ingredients used to prepare it. Mild chile peppers are used in the Yucatán region, while spicier chiles are preferred on the east coast and in central Mexico.

. . . .

2 tablespoons vegetable oil
8 ounces (225 g) pork loin, cubed
½ teaspoon ground black pepper
½ teaspoon ground cumin
2 tablespoons chopped yellow (brown) onion
2 cups (1 lb 2 oz/500 g) Homemade Roasted Tomatillo Salsa (see page 27)
½ cup (2½ oz/75 g) cooked yellow corn kernels
1 teaspoon dried oregano
10 corn tortillas
Sea salt, to taste

Toppings
Mexican Blistered Chiles (see page 52), cut into slices
Pineapple Pico de Gallo (see page 38)

Heat the oil in a lidded skillet or frying pan over a medium-high heat, add the pork, and season with the black pepper, cumin, and salt. Sear the meat for about 1 minute on all sides, until browned.

Add the onion to the pan and sauté, stirring occasionally, until translucent.

Add the tomatillo salsa, then reduce the heat to medium, cover with a lid, and let simmer for 15 to 20 minutes. Add the corn kernels and oregano, and taste and adjust the salt, if necessary. Let simmer for 3 to 4 minutes until the corn has been heated.

Meanwhile, briefly heat the tortillas on a comal or flat griddle (grill) pan to warm them, then build your taco, filling the tortillas with the stew and adding the toppings.

Although pork plays a large role in Mexican cuisine, the pigs that supply the meat did not arrive in Mexico and the New World until the early sixteenth century, when the Spanish explorer Hernán Cortés introduced Iberian, Neapolitan, and Celtic pigs to Mexico, where they became wild. New breeds have since arrived, and Mexico is among the world's leading producers of pork.

COCHINITA PIBIL

PULLED PORK

MAKES 10

The traditional Mexican cochinita pibil recipe is from the Yucatán
Peninsula, where a *cochinita*, or suckling pig, is marinated in a
strong acidic citrus juice. Following the traditional recipe is very
labor intensive and requires a lot of cooking time, so here's a simple
and quicker way to prepare this rich dish. If you struggle to find
fresh banana leaves, cover the pot with aluminum foil instead.

2½ lbs (1 kg) pork butt or shoulder
Banana leaves, about 24 inches
 (60 cm) square
10 corn or flour tortillas
Sea salt and freshly ground black
 pepper, to taste

Marinade
4 cloves garlic, peeled
½ yellow (brown) onion
1 habanero chile (you can remove the
 seeds and membrane to reduce
 the heat)
½ cup achiote paste
1 teaspoon ground cumin
1 teaspoon dried oregano
¼ teaspoon ground cinnamon
¼ cup (2 fl oz/60 ml) lime juice
¼ cup (2 fl oz/60 ml) orange juice
4 cups (1¾ pints/1 liter) chicken broth
 (stock)

Toppings
Pickled Red Onions (see page 56)
Serrano-Cucumber Salsa (see page 36)

Preheat the oven to 350°F (180°C/Gas Mark 4).

Make the marinade. In a sauté pan over a medium-high heat,
dry-roast the garlic, onion, and habanero for 3 to 5 minutes. When
they are charred, remove from the pan and let cool, then transfer
them to a blender. Add the remaining marinade ingredients and
blend until smooth.

Cut the pork butt or shoulder into pieces and season with salt.

If you are using the banana leaves, lay them in a Dutch oven,
deep casserole dish, or roasting pan large enough to hold the
meat and with enough room to fold in the leaves to cover the top.
Place the pork over the leaves and season with salt and pepper.

Pour the marinade over the pork and massage it in so that it is
evenly coated. Fold the banana leaves and tuck them down the
sides. Alternatively, cover the top tightly with aluminum foil.

Bake in the preheated over for 2 hours, then check for
tenderness—the pork should fall apart when pulled with a fork.
If it does not easily shred, return it to the oven for an additional
30 to 40 minutes or until you obtain the desired consistency.
Shred the pork by pulling it apart with two forks.

Briefly heat the tortillas on a comal or flat griddle (grill) pan to
warm them, then build your taco, filling the tortillas with the
pork and adding the toppings.

CARNE ASADA
GRILLED STEAK

MAKES 6

Enjoying the aromas of marinated steak over the grill is one of my favorite experiences during summer. But don't worry, this recipe allows you to conquer this delicious dish in the comfort of your kitchen too. The longer you give the beef to marinate, the better—so let's get marinating!

1 lb (450 g) hanger or skirt steak
1 tablespoon vegetable oil
1½ teaspoons salt
1 teaspoon ground black pepper
¼ yellow (brown) onion, minced
1 tablespoon minced garlic
2 tablespoons minced fresh
   jalapeño chile
¼ cup (2 fl oz/60 ml) lime juice
¼ cup (2 fl oz/60 ml) orange juice
2 tablespoons salsa inglesa,
   Worcestershire sauce, or soy sauce
1 cup (8 fl oz/240 ml) Mexican beer
6 corn or flour tortillas

Toppings
Grilled scallions (spring onions)
Mexican Blistered Chiles (see page 52)

Rub the steak with the oil, salt, and black pepper. Place the meat in a resealable bag, add the onion, garlic, and jalapeño, and pour in the lime juice, orange juice, salsa inglesa, and beer. Make sure the marinade is covering all of the meat, then let it sit for at least 1 hour.

Put a comal, flat griddle (grill) pan, or cast-iron skillet or frying pan over high heat. Lay the steak in the pan and let sear for 2 minutes, then repeat for the other side. Reduce the heat to medium and continue to cook for 4 to 6 minutes. Transfer the steak to a cutting (chopping) board. Let it rest for 6 minutes, then cut it into strips against the grain.

Briefly heat the tortillas on the comal or flat griddle pan to warm them, then build your taco, filling the tortillas with the beef and adding the toppings.

To make grilled scallions, cut them in half lengthwise. When you remove the steak from the pan, put the scallions in and char on both sides, then squeeze lime juice over and season with salt. Alternatively, cook them under a broiler or on an outdoor grill rack.

PICADILLO NORTEÑO
NORTHERN GROUND BEEF STEW

MAKES 10

Picadillo, comprising ground meat in a tomato sauce, is a favorite dish in Latin American countries. In Mexico, the beef version is a popular *antojito*, or street food, that often includes carrots and potatoes—but there are regional variations, such as those including squash or peas.

1 cup (8 fl oz/240 ml) chicken broth (stock)
4 tomatoes, quartered
1 teaspoon dried oregano
1 teaspoon ground cumin
1 teaspoon paprika
2 teaspoons salt
1 teaspoon ground black pepper
3 tablespoons vegetable oil
3 cloves garlic, peeled
½ onion, quartered, plus ¼ cup (1½ oz/45 g) minced onion
¼ cup (¾ oz/20 g) minced jalapeño chiles
1 lb (450 g) ground (minced) beef
1 cup (5 oz/150 g) diced potatoes
½ cup (2½ oz/75 g) diced carrots
½ cup (½ oz/15 g) chopped fresh cilantro (coriander)
Juice of 1 lime
10 flour tortillas
Plain or Mexican rice, to serve

Toppings
Chopped fresh cilantro (coriander)
Homemade Roasted Tomatillo Salsa (optional; see page 27)
Queso fresco or feta cheese, crumbled (optional)
Shredded lettuce (optional)

In a blender, add the chicken broth or stock, tomatoes, oregano, cumin, paprika, salt, and black pepper, then blend until smooth.

Heat the oil in a wide skillet over a medium-high heat. When hot, add the garlic, onions, and jalapeños, and sauté, stirring occasionally, for 3 to 5 minutes, until the onion is translucent.

Add the ground beef to the pan and break it up with a wooden spoon as it cooks. When crumbled, pour in the tomato broth and let it come to a simmer, then add the potatoes and carrots. Reduce the heat to medium and let simmer, stirring occasionally, for 8 to 10 minutes. Stir in the fresh cilantro and lime juice.

Briefly heat the tortillas on a comal or flat griddle (grill) pan to warm them, then build your taco, filling the tortillas with the beef and adding the toppings, as desired. Serve with Mexican rice on the side.

ALAMBRES

BEEF SKEWERS

MAKES 10

The Spanish word *alambre* means "wire" in English, probably referring to the skewers used to cook the meat for the Mexican dish, which is especially popular in Mexico City and Oaxaca. If you are using wooden skewers, soak them in water for at least 5 minutes before using so they don't burn. You can also make this recipe using chicken or pork.

1 lb (450 g) sirloin (rump) steak, cut into 1½-inch (4-cm) pieces
4 tablespoons vegetable oil
½ cup (4 fl oz/120 ml) salsa inglesa, Worcestershire sauce, or soy sauce
1 red onion, cut into 2-inch (5-cm) squares
2 green, orange or red bell peppers, cut into 2-inch (5-cm) squares
1–2 zucchini (courgettes), sliced into 1-inch (2.5-cm) rounds
1½ teaspoons garlic powder
1½ teaspoons chile powder
1½ teaspoons dry thyme
10 corn or flour tortillas
Sea salt and freshly ground black pepper, to taste

Toppings
Salsa of your choice
Lime slices or wedges

Prepare your barbecue and grease the grill rack.

In a mixing bowl, add the beef, 2 tablespoons of the vegetable oil, the salsa inglesa, salt, and black pepper. Mix it all together well.

In a separate mixing bowl, add the onion, bell peppers, and zucchini. Add the remaining 2 tablespoons of oil, the garlic powder, chile powder, thyme, salt, and black pepper. Mix it all together well.

Grab 10 skewers and start layering the meat and vegetable pieces in your preferred order.

Lay the skewers on the grill rack, and turn every 6 minutes, until the internal temperature of the beef reaches 145°F (63°C) on a meat thermometer; if you don't have a thermometer, cut into a piece with a sharp knife to check for doneness. When ready, let the skewers rest for 6 minutes.

Meanwhile, briefly heat the tortillas over the grill rack or on a comal or flat griddle (grill) pan, then slide the ingredients off the skewers with your fingers or a fork. Fill the tortillas with the beef and vegetables. Top with salsa and a squeeze of lime.

This is one of several recipes in this book that uses salsa inglesa, a bottled sauce often found on tables in Mexican restaurants. The sweet-and-sour sauce tastes exactly like Worcestershire sauce.

POLLO POBLANO
CHICKEN IN POBLANO SAUCE

MAKES 10

This chicken dish uses poblano chiles, named after the Mexican state of Puebla, where it is thought they were first grown. The dark green poblano chiles (which are ancho chiles when dried) are popular in Mexican cuisine, because they add a great deal of flavor without too much heat, especially when roasted—as in this recipe!

6 fresh poblano chiles
1 cup (8 fl oz/240 ml) chicken broth (stock)
1 cup (8 fl oz/240 ml) heavy (double) cream
½ cup (4 oz/115 g) cream cheese
2 tablespoons (2 oz/55 g) butter or vegetable oil
½ white or yellow (brown) onion, sliced into strips
1 tablespoon minced garlic
4 cups (1¼ lbs/575 g) shredded cooked chicken
½ cup (2½ oz/75 g) corn kernels
10 corn or flour tortillas

Topping
Chopped fresh cilantro (coriander)

Preheat the broiler (grill) to high.

Lay the whole poblano chiles in the broiler (grill) pan and put it under the heat, rotating the chiles every couple of minutes until the skins turn black on all sides. When blackened, put them into a sealable bag or container to lock in the steam (this will make them easier to peel them). Let them sit for 15 minutes.

Using a clean kitchen towel to hold them, rub off the skin. Cut the stems off and remove the seeds. Slice the poblanos into ¼-inch (6-mm)-thick strips.

In a blender, add the chicken broth or stock, heavy cream, cream cheese, and half of the sliced poblanos. Blend until smooth.

Melt the butter or heat the oil in a wide skillet or frying pan over a medium-high heat, then add the onion and garlic. Sauté, stirring occasionally, until the onion is a little translucent, then add the poblano sauce. Reduce the heat to medium—do not let the sauce boil or it will split.

When the sauce starts to turn a darker green, add the chicken, corn, and remaining poblano peppers. Cover and let simmer for 10 minutes.

Briefly heat the tortillas on a comal or flat griddle (grill) pan to warm them, then build your taco, filling the tortillas with the chicken and its sauce, and scattering over cilantro.

TINGA DE POLLO
CHICKEN IN CHIPOTLE SAUCE

MAKES 10

This popular dish, which first appeared in the Puebla region during the colonial period, combines Spanish and Mexican ingredients: shredded chicken in a tangy, spicy sauce. Since then, it has spread throughout Mexico, perhaps because it's a quick and easy dish to prepare—and after you've had it once, you'll want it again and again!

2 tablespoons vegetable oil
½ onion, cut into ¼-in (6-mm) strips
1 tablespoon minced garlic
2 red or orange bell peppers, cut into ¼-in (6-mm) strips
1 cup (8 fl oz/240 ml) chicken broth (stock)
¼ cup (2 fl oz/60 ml) morita or chipotle purée or paste
4 cups (1¼ lbs/575 g) shredded cooked chicken
2 cups (12 oz/350 g) diced tomatoes
10 corn or flour tortillas

Toppings
Sliced scallions (spring onions)
Pico de gallo (see box page 38)
Queso fresco or feta cheese, crumbled
Street Taco Salsa (see page 28)
Lime wedges

Heat the vegetable oil in a wide skillet or frying pan over a medium-high heat. When hot, add the onion, garlic, and bell peppers, and sauté, stirring occasionally, until they start to caramelize.

Deglaze with the chicken broth or stock, add the chipotle sauce, and let simmer for 10 minutes.

Add the chicken and tomatoes, cover with a lid, and continue to let simmer for 10 minutes.

Briefly heat the tortillas on a comal or flat griddle (grill) pan to warm them, then build your taco, filling the tortillas with the chicken and toppings and drizzling over the salsa.

Chipotles in adobo is used in several of the recipes in this book, where it is referred to as chipotle purée or paste. You may find it labeled as chipotle morita paste or see it called chipotle sauce in recipes (not to be confused with chipotle or morita mayonnaise). Most cooks use the canned or jar varieties rather than making homemade versions.

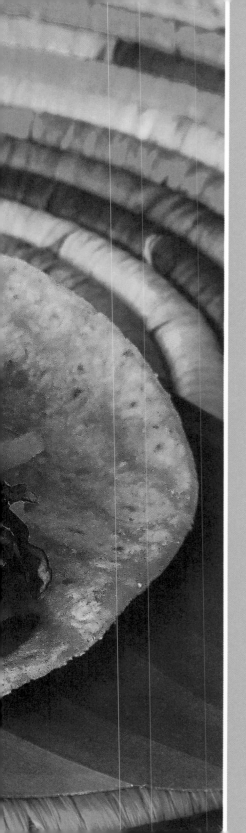

5

Fish and Seafood

Fish and seafood dishes are particularly popular
along the coasts of Mexico, where they have
been eating fish tacos for centuries!

There are many traditional recipes from
the Gulf as well as from the Pacific and Baja
California regions, and in this chapter you will
find a fantastic variety of tacos from all over.
Try the gobernador from the Pacific, the red
snapper from Veracruz, or the deviled shrimp
tacos from Acapulco.

CAMARONES A LA DIABLA

MEXICAN DEVILED SHRIMP

MAKES 6

A coastal dish that is very popular in Acapulco, the fiery red chile sauce marries well with the juiciness of the seafood in these diablo shrimp. You can also prepare jumbo shrimp in this sauce and serve them as an appetizer.

4 guajillo chiles, stems and seeds removed
2 chiles de árbol, stems and seeds removed
2 small roma (plum) tomatoes
4 cloves garlic, peeled
2 tablespoons vegetable oil
1 lb (450 g) shrimp (prawns), peeled and deveined (reserve the shells)
½ onion, cut into strips
1 red or orange bell pepper, cut into strips
Juice of ½ lime
6 corn tortillas
Sea salt and freshly ground black pepper, to taste

Toppings
Shredded red cabbage
Fresh cilantro (coriander) leaves
Queso fresco or feta cheese, crumbled
Lime wedges

Place the guajillo chiles in a mixing bowl, pour boiling hot water over them, and let sit for 6 minutes.

When the chiles are soft, transfer to a blender or food processor, add the tomatoes and garlic and, if you have the shrimp shells, also add them. Add ½ cup of water, season with salt and black pepper, and blend until smooth. Strain through a colander and set aside.

Heat the oil in a skillet or frying pan over a medium–high heat. Add the shrimp, onion, and bell pepper and sauté for 2 to 3 minutes, until the shrimp start to turn slightly pink. Add the sauce and let simmer for 5 to 8 minutes or until sauce thickens.

Turn off the heat and squeeze lime over the top to add freshness.

Heat the tortillas on a comal or flat griddle (grill) pan, then place the shrimp in the tortillas and add the toppings.

You may leave the black veins in small shrimp but in larger ones they can have an unpleasant gritty texture. To peel and devein a shrimp, first pull off the head, if still attached, and the legs. To remove the shells, start at the head end and pull off the shell. Use the tip of a sharp knife to remove the vein that runs under the surface of the back.

GOBERNADOR
SHRIMP AND CHEESE

MAKES 10

The story behind these tacos is that they get their name from a Sinaloan governor, who enjoyed them while visiting a restaurant in Mazatlán, where the owners named this dish after him—*tacos gobernador* means "governor's tacos" in English. This shrimp and cheese combination is also popular in the Baja California region.

1 poblano chile or bell pepper
2 tablespoons vegetable oil
2 tablespoons minced red onion
1 tablespoon minced garlic
½ celery stalk, cut into thin slices
1 lb (450 g) shrimp (prawns), peeled and deveined
½ cup (2 oz/60 g) shredded Manchego cheese, mozzarella, or Monterey Jack
10 flour or corn tortillas

Toppings
Sliced scallion (spring onion)
Pico de gallo (see box page 38)
Avocado Crema (see page 32)
Lime wedges

Dry-roast the poblano chile or bell pepper over an open fire or on a broiler (grill) pan under a high heat until the skin chars. Place the chile or pepper in a sealable food bag, seal, and let steam for 5 to 6 minutes. Remove and rub off the burned skin with a clean kitchen towel. Cut the flesh into small squares.

Add the oil to a skillet or frying pan over a medium-high heat, heat briefly, then add the onion, garlic, and celery. When the onion and celery are translucent, add the shrimp and charred chile or bell pepper and sauté for about 3 minutes, until the shrimp turns pink and is cooked.

Add the shredded cheese on top and decrease the heat. Heat the tortillas on a comal or flat griddle (grill) pan. When the cheese has melted, transfer the filling to the tortillas. Top with the scallion and pico de gallo and drizzle over the avocado crema. Finish with a squeeze of lime.

CAMARÓN Y PIÑA
SHRIMP AND PINEAPPLE

MAKES 6

Pineapple can often be found in Mexican cuisine, in both savory and sweet dishes, and you can often see the fruit cooking above the meat spit roast in restaurants and street stands, particularly in Oaxaca, the Pineapple Capital of the World. These delicious shrimp tacos make a quick and tasty meal, with the pineapple adding tangy sweetness.

1½ lbs (675 g) shrimp (prawns), peeled and deveined
2 tablespoons vegetable oil
Sea salt and freshly ground black pepper, to taste
6 corn tortillas

Toppings
Sliced avocado
Morita Mayonnaise (see page 31)
Pineapple Pico de Gallo (see page 38)
Shredded cabbage or lettuce (optional)

In a mixing bowl, mix the shrimp (prawns) with the vegetable oil, and season with salt and black pepper.

Heat a comal or flat griddle (grill) pan over a medium-high heat. Add the shrimp to the pan and turn over when they turn pink and opaque. Remove the shrimp from the pan

Briefly heat the tortillas on a clean comal or flat griddle pan to warm them.

Build your taco, first filling the tortillas with the shrimp. Next, layer on the avocado. Drizzle the morita mayonnaise over the top and sprinkle with the pineapple pico de gallo. Finish with shredded cabbage or lettuce for extra freshness, if desired.

PESCADO BORRACHO
FRIED FISH

MAKES 6

There is little doubt that fish wrapped in tortillas have been enjoyed along the Mexican coastal areas for many years, but this more modern version of deep-fried fish served with a creamy mayonnaise-based topping dates back to only about the 1950s or 1960s. There is a debate about whether its origins are in the coastal towns of Ensenada or San Felipe—but there's no debate about how delicious it is!

Vegetable oil, for frying
2 medium-size red snapper, tilapia,
    or cod fillets, cut into 6 strips
Sea salt and freshly ground black
    pepper, to taste
6 corn or flour tortillas

Batter
½ cup (65 g) flour, plus extra for dusting
2 teaspoons baking powder
1 tablespoon cornstarch (cornflour)
2 teaspoons salt
2 teaspoons ground black pepper
1 teaspoon paprika
1 teaspoon garlic powder
1 egg
1 cup (8 fl oz/240 ml) Mexican beer

Toppings
Morita Mayonnaise (see page 31)
Shredded red cabbage
Pineapple Pico de Gallo (see page 38)

First make the batter. In a mixing bowl, mix the flour with the baking powder, cornstarch, salt, pepper, paprika, and garlic powder.

In a separate mixing bowl, beat the egg, then mix it into the dry mixture. Slowly start to add the beer while whisking it into the batter. Set aside.

In a deep fryer or large pot, heat the oil for frying to 350°F (180°C), or until a cube of bread browns in 30 seconds.

Meanwhile, pat the fish fillets dry with paper towels and season with salt and pepper. Dust the fillets in flour and then dip them into the batter.

When the oil is at 350°F (180°C), drop in two fillets at a time—don't overcrowd the oil or the temperature will drop. When golden brown, transfer the fish to a cooling rack or on paper towels to drain.

Briefly heat the tortillas on a comal or flat griddle (grill) pan, then build your taco, placing a fish fillet in each one. Drizzle with morita mayonnaise and top with the shredded red cabbage and pineapple pico de gallo.

PESCADO A LA VERACRUZANA

VERACRUZ-STYLE FISH

MAKES 4

As its name suggests, this dish originated in the Mexican state of Veracruz, which, being on the Gulf of Mexico, has easy access to fishing. This recipe is an easier version of the traditional recipe, which would involve baking a whole *huachinango*, or red snapper, in the oven. If you don't have red snapper on hand, any firm white fish, such as tilapia, sea bass, or cod, can be used as a substitute. Regardless of the white fish you use, it's guaranteed to be delectable!

2 small red snapper, tilapia, or cod fillets
2 tablespoons vegetable oil
4 corn tortillas
Sea salt and freshly ground black
    pepper, to taste

Sauce
2 tablespoons olive oil
½ white onion, diced
3 cloves garlic, peeled and minced
1 yellow or orange bell pepper, roasted,
    peeled, and cut into pieces
1 serrano chile, minced
½ cup (4 fl oz/120 ml) white wine
1 tomato, diced
1 bay leaf
1 tablespoon butter
¼ cup (1 ½ oz/45 g) sliced, pitted
    green olives

Toppings
Fresh epazote or basil leaves
Lime wedges

For the sauce, heat a sauté pan over a medium-high temperature, then add the olive oil and swirl it around. Add the onion and cook for 2 to 3 minutes, until translucent, then add the garlic, bell pepper, and serrano. Sauté for about 1 minute, then deglaze with the white wine. Bring it to a simmer and add the diced tomato and bay leaf. Reduce the heat to medium and cover for 5 minutes. Finish by stirring in the butter and olive slices.

Season the fish fillets with salt and pepper.

Heat the vegetable oil in a nonstick skillet or frying pan over a medium-high heat. When the oil is hot, cook the fillets for 2 to 3 minutes on each side, carefully flipping with a fish spatula.

Heat the tortillas on a comal or flat griddle (grill) pan, then build your taco, placing a fish fillet in each one and topping with the Veracruz-style sauce, fresh epazote leaves, and a squeeze of lime.

I love adding fresh epazote leaves to this dish. This herb, which is popular in central and southern Mexican cuisine, has a strong flavor and aroma with hints of oregano, anise, citrus, and mint, but also tar. It can be an acquired taste—the name, taken from the Nahuatl language, means "stinky sweat"—but it adds a rustic flavor.

TOSTADA DE ATÚN

TUNA TOSTADA

MAKES 4

Given that sesame seeds are native to Africa and India, these tiny round seeds are surprisingly popular in Mexican cuisine, and they are often found in salsas, salads, and desserts. Here is another example of Mexican cuisine adopting an Old World ingredient. These seeds work well with chiles, and toasting them brings out their rich, nutty flavor.

2 tuna fillets
1 tablespoon sesame oil
Vegetable oil, for frying
1 tablespoon Mexican Chile Oil (see page 33); straining as much of the oil as you can, or chile paste
2 tablespoons mayonnaise
½ cup (2 oz/60 g) toasted black and white sesame seeds, plus extra to garnish
4 corn tortillas
Sea salt and freshly ground black pepper, to taste

Toppings
Shredded red cabbage
Cucumber slices
Habanero chile slices
Sliced scallion (spring onion)
Toasted sesame seeds
Lime wedges

Heat a comal or flat griddle (grill) pan over a medium-high heat. Preheat the oven to 400°F (200°C/Gas mark 6).

Pat dry the tuna with paper towels, then rub them with the sesame oil, and season with salt and pepper.

Brush a little vegetable oil on the comal or griddle (grill pan) and lay the tuna fillets in the pan. Cook each side for about 2 minutes (depending on size) and about 30 seconds on the edges. You want to just sear the edges and leave the middle rare. Remove the fish from the pan, and let rest for about 2 minutes.

In a mixing bowl, mix the chile oil and mayonnaise until well combined. Slice the tuna fillets into thin rectangles, cutting against the grain, and coat each one in the sesame seeds.

To make tostadas, bake the tortillas in the oven for 5 to 8 minutes on each side until crispy (or pan fry them in vegetable oil). Spread the mayonnaise on the tostadas and lay 3 to 4 pieces of tuna on top of each. Add the cabbage and cucumber, then finish with a chile slices, if using, scallion, sesame seeds, and a squeeze of lime juice.

To toast the sesame seeds, heat them in a dry skillet or frying pan over a medium-low heat, stirring occasionally, for 2 to 3 minutes, until the seeds turn brown and shiny and start to pop. For more flavor, bake them in a preheated oven at 350°F (175°C/Gas Mark 4) for 8 to 15 minutes, until lightly brown. Shake the pan every few minutes and keep an eye on them, because sesame seeds can burn quickly.

CHICHARRÓN DE PESCADO

CRISPY FISH

MAKES 6

**Popular as a snack food and sold in markets and by street
vendors, there are many variations to the ingredients that
make up chicharrones. This version wraps cubes of fried fish
in tortillas with guacamole and pickled red onions.**

Vegetable oil, for frying
2 red snapper fillets, cut into
    large cubes
½ cup (2 oz/60 g) all-purpose
    (plain) flour
½ cup (2 oz/60 g) cornstarch
    (cornflour)
1 teaspoon garlic powder
1 teaspoon chile powder or paprika
2 teaspoons salt
2 eggs
1 teaspoon ground white pepper
6 corn tortillas

Toppings
Guacamole (see page 54)
Pickled Red Onions (see page 56)
Shredded red cabbage
Morita Mayonnaise (see page 31)
Lime wedges

Fill a deep pot with the vegetable oil and heat until it reaches
375°F (190°C) on a thermometer or until a cube of bread browns
in 30 seconds.

Meanwhile, in a mixing bowl, mix the flour with the cornstarch
(cornflour), garlic powder, chile powder, and salt. In a separate
mixing bowl, beat the two eggs.

Pat dry the fish fillets with paper towels and cut them into large
cubes. Season the cubes with white ground pepper, dust them
with the flour mixture until evenly coated, and then dredge them
in the egg mixture.

Dredge the fish cubes in the flour mixture again and carefully
start frying them, a few at a time to avoid lowering the oil
temperature. Fry for 2 to 3 minutes until golden brown, then
transfer to a wire cooling rack.

While the fish is cooling, briefly heat the tortillas on a comal or
flat griddle (grill) pan to warm them. Spread the tortillas with the
guacamole and top with the fish chicharrones. Add the toppings,
drizzling the salsa over the top.

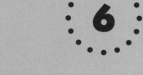

6

Vegan and Vegetarian

With its reliance on fresh vegetables, fruit, mushrooms, beans, corn, and nuts and seeds, Mexican is one of the best cuisines for a vegetarian diet.

On the following pages you will find cheese-stuffed peppers, mushroom fajitas and tinga, cauliflower al pastor—all classic authentic Mexican favorites but in meat-free versions. Many of the vegetarian recipes can be made vegan by omitting the cheese and crema, or by substituting a vegan Mexican cheese such as queso fresco or cotija.

CHILE RELLENO
STUFFED CHILE PEPPER

MAKES 4

This stuffed pepper dish is a Mexican favorite that first appeared in the city of Puebla. A nineteenth-century description notes that it consisted of a "green chile pepper stuffed with meat and coated in eggs." Our vegetarian version is also popular in Mexico, often with queso Chihuahua, a mild cheese made of cow milk that is similar to cheddar cheese.

4 poblano chiles
1 cup (4 oz/115 g) shredded cheese, such as Chihuahua, cheddar, or Monterey Jack
4 corn or flour tortillas
Sea salt and freshly ground black pepper, to taste

Toppings
Caramelized onions
Charred tomatoes
Homemade Red Salsa (see page 26)
Pineapple Pico de Gallo (see page 38) (optional)
Mexican crema or sour cream (optional)

Dry-roast the poblano chiles over an open flame on the stove (hob) or under the broiler (grill), turning them occasionally, until the skin is charred and blackened all over. Place the charred chiles in a bowl, covered with plastic wrap (clingfilm), for 8 to 10 minutes—the steam will make it easier to remove the skin.

Meanwhile, preheat the oven to 350°F (180°/Gas Mark 4).

Remove the skins from the chiles by rubbing them with a clean kitchen towel, being careful not to tear them—you need them whole.

Carefully make an incision in the middle of the chiles and remove as many seeds as you can. Through the same openings, stuff the cheese inside the chiles, then place them on a baking sheet and season with salt and black pepper.

Cook the chiles in the preheated oven for about 5 minute or until the cheese melts. Remove and let cool for about 3 minutes.

Meanwhile, briefly heat the tortillas on a comal or flat griddle (grill) pan to warm them.

Carefully remove the chiles from the baking sheet and place one on top of each tortilla. Keep building your tacos, topping them with the caramelized onions, charred tomatoes, red salsa, and other toppings of your choice.

This recipe calls for poblanos, but you can substitute other large chiles, such as jalapeños, banana chiles, or Anaheim chiles. *Chiles en nogada* is a version served with a walnut cream sauce and pomegranate seeds.

RAJAS CON QUESO

ROASTED POBLANO AND CHEESE

MAKES 6

The Mexican word *rajas* means "strips," referring to the strips of poblano chiles served in this cheese sauce, which is also made with corn kernels and Mexican crema. If you can't find Mexican crema, you can substitute it, along with the milk (which is used to thin it), with heavy (double) cream.

4 large poblano chiles
1 tablespoon butter
½ onion, sliced lengthwise into ½-inch (12-mm) strips
4 cloves garlic, peeled and minced
½ cup (2½ oz/70 g) cooked yellow corn kernels
1 cup (8 fl oz/240 ml) Mexican crema or crème fraîche
½ cup (4 fl oz/120 ml) milk
½ cup (2 oz/60 g) shredded quesillo cheese, Monterey Jack, or cheddar cheese
6 corn or flour tortillas
Sea salt and freshly ground black pepper, to taste

Toppings
Chopped fresh cilantro (coriander)
Shredded quesillo cheese, Monterey Jack, or cheddar cheese

Dry-roast the poblano chiles over an open flame on the stove (hob) or under the broiler (grill), turning them occasionally, until the skin is charred and blackened all over. Place the charred chiles in a bowl, covered with plastic wrap (clingfilm), for 8 to 10 minutes—the steam will make it easier to remove the skin.

Remove the skins from the chiles by rubbing them with a clean kitchen towel. Slice open the chile, then cut the cap off, remove the seeds, and cut into ½-inch (12-mm) strips.

Melt the butter in a skillet or frying pan set over a medium heat, then add the onion and garlic. Stir occasionally until the onion starts to become translucent, then add the chiles and corn, followed by the crema, milk, and cheese. Season with salt and black pepper and stir until it is well combined. Let simmer for 8 to 10 minutes, until the mixture is thick. Make sure the heat does not get too high or the cream will separate or burn.

Briefly heat the tortillas on a comal or flat griddle (grill) pan to warm them, then begin building your tacos, starting with the poblano chile-and-cheese sauce and finishing with a sprinkling of cheese and fresh cilantro.

TINGA DE HONGOS
SHREDDED MUSHROOMS IN CHIPOTLE SAUCE

MAKES 6

Originally from the Puebla region, *tinga* (which means "vulgar" or "messy") normally consists of shredded chicken with sliced onion in a tomato and chipotle chile marinade, but this vegetarian version replaces the chicken with mushrooms, giving this dish a rich, earthy flavor. To make this a vegan dish, omit the Mexican crema and queso fresco.

2 tomatoes
½ cup (4 fl oz/120 ml) vegetable broth (stock)
2 tablespoons chipotle purée or paste
2 cloves garlic, peeled
2 tablespoons vegetable oil
½ white or yellow (brown) onion, sliced lengthwise into ¼-inch (6-mm) strips
1 yellow, red, or green bell pepper, sliced into ½-inch (12-mm) strips
1 lb (450 g) mushrooms, (lion's mane, oyster, crimini/chestnut, shiitake, portobello/field), shredded into ½-inch (12-mm) pieces
6 tortillas
Sea salt and freshly ground black pepper, to taste

Toppings
Mexican crema or sour cream
Queso fresco or feta cheese, crumbled
Fresh cilantro (coriander) leaves

Add the tomatoes, vegetable broth (stock), chipotle purée, and garlic to a blender and blend until smooth.

Heat a large skillet or frying pan over a medium-high heat, then add the vegetable oil and swirl it around. Add the onion and bell pepper strips, and sauté for about 5 minutes, until the onion starts to brown.

Add the shredded mushrooms, stir, and then add the tomato sauce mixture. Season with salt and black pepper, and let simmer for 8 to 10 minutes.

Briefly heat the tortillas on a comal or flat griddle (grill) pan to warm them, then begin building your tacos, starting with the tinga, followed by the Mexican crema or sour cream, queso fresco or feta, and fresh cilantro.

To prepare the mushrooms, press the tines of a fork into the flesh and pull to shred it (if the mushrooms have large caps, you may want to first separate them from the stems/stalks and quarter them). You can pull apart larger shreds with your hands to make them smaller, and it's perfectly fine if the mushrooms break up into chunks, which will add texture. Alternatively, slice the mushrooms thinly.

PAPAS A LA MACHA
ROASTED POTATOES AND CHILE OIL

MAKES 6

These *papas*, or potatoes, are prepared a la Mexicana style—in a *salsa macha* with chiles and onions. The tacos are perfect for breakfast, lunch, or dinner, and can be accompanied with refried beans for a more substantial meal. To make this a vegan taco, omit the avocado crema and cheese.

4 small red potatoes, peeled and cut ½-inch (12-mm) cubes
1 large carrot, cut into ½-inch (12-mm) rounds
¼ cup (2 fl oz/60 ml) Mexican Chile Oil (see page 33)
¼ cup (2 fl oz/60 ml) vegetable oil
2 teaspoons salt
6 corn or flour tortillas

Toppings
Avocado Crema (see page 32)
Sliced scallions (spring onions)
Fresh cilantro (coriander) leaves

Preheat the oven to 350°F (180°C/Gas Mark 4).

In a mixing bowl, add the potatoes, carrots, chile oil, vegetable oil, and salt. Mix until the potatoes and carrots are evenly coated.

Evenly spread the vegetables on a baking sheet and bake in the preheated oven for 15 to 20 minutes.

Briefly heat the tortillas on a comal or flat griddle (grill) pan to warm them, then begin building your tacos, starting with the avocado crema, then the potatoes in the chile oil and sprinkling over sliced scallions and cilantro, if desired.

PORTOBELLO FAJITAS
SIZZLING MUSHROOMS

MAKES 6

Fajitas, which means "little belt or sash," are thought to have been first prepared in the mid-twentieth century by Mexican workers on ranches in Texas, who were given leftover strips of beef as part of their pay. Today, fajitas usually consist of onion and bell peppers marinated with meat, but mushrooms replace the latter here to make this a vegetarian taco. For a vegan version, use a vegan plant-based sour cream or crème fraîche.

. . . .

2 large portobello (field) caps, cut into ½-inch (12-mm) strips
½ white onion, cut lengthwise into ½-inch (12-mm) strips
1 orange bell pepper, cut into ½-inch (12-mm) strips
1½ teaspoons ground cumin
1½ teaspoons chile powder
1 tablespoon minced garlic
1 tablespoon minced ginger
2 tablespoons vegetable oil
6 corn or flour tortillas
Sea salt and freshly ground black pepper, to taste

Toppings
Stone Mortar Salsa (see page 30)
Guacamole (see page 54)
Pico de gallo (see box page 38)
Mexican crema, sour cream, or vegan plain yogurt
Fresh cilantro (coriander) leaves
Lime wedges

In a large mixing bowl, add the portobello mushrooms, onion, bell pepper, cumin, chile powder, garlic, ginger, and oil. Season with salt and black pepper. Mix it all together with your hands until everything is evenly coated. Let marinate for 5 to 10 minutes.

Heat a large skillet or frying pan over a high heat. When it is hot, carefully add the mushroom mixture. Let cook, without stirring, for 1 minute to sear well, then stir everything well and cook again, without stirring, for another 1 minute. Reduce the temperature to medium.

Briefly heat the tortillas on a comal or flat griddle (grill) pan to warm them.

Serve the mushroom mixture and tortillas separately on a tray or platter with the various toppings to let each diner build his or her own fajita.

MILANESA DE BERENJENA CON COL
EGGPLANT MILANESA WITH COLESLAW

MAKES 6

The Spanish thought the eggplant (aubergine) was an aphrodisiac, which is why they named it *berengenas*, or "apple of love," but Albert of Cologne referred to it as *mala insana*, or "mad apples," because it was thought to lead to insanity. The Spanish introduced the eggplant to Mexico around 1650, and regardless of its history, it is a popular ingredient in Mexican cuisine. In this recipe it works perfectly with the coleslaw.

1 eggplant (aubergine)
1 cup (4½ oz/125 g) all-purpose (plain) flour
2 eggs, beaten
1 cup (3½ oz/100 g) dry breadcrumbs
2 teaspoons salt
1 teaspoon ground black pepper
1 teaspoon garlic powder
1 teaspoon onion powder
1 teaspoon chile powder
1 cup (8 fl oz/240 ml) vegetable oil
6 corn or blue corn tortillas
Sliced scallions (spring onions) and jalapeños, to garnish
Pickled Vegetables (see page 58)

Coleslaw
1 cup (3½ oz/100 g) shredded cabbage
¼ cup (1 oz/25 g) shredded carrots
1 teaspoon lime juice
1 teaspoon apple cider vinegar
2–3 tablespoons Morita Mayonnaise (see page 31), chipotle mayonnaise, or regular mayonnaise
Sea salt and freshly ground black pepper, to taste

Slice both ends off the eggplant. Then cut in half widthwise and then again lengthwise into 6 steaks, ½-inch (12-mm) thick.

Set up three plates for breading the eggplant—for the flour, the beaten eggs, and the breadcrumbs. Season the eggplant with salt, pepper, and garlic, onion, and chile powder. One by one, start breading by patting the eggplant with flour, coating it with egg, and then pressing it into the breadcrumbs on both sides. Set on a baking tray in a single layer and let sit for 10 to 20 minutes.

In a large mixing bowl, add all the coleslaw ingredients, mix well to combine, and season to taste. Cover and refrigerate.

Heat a large skillet or frying pan over a medium-high heat. Add the vegetable oil for pan frying. Once hot, carefully place your eggplant in the oil and sear until golden on both sides.

Briefly heat the tortillas on a comal or flat griddle (grill) pan to warm them. Add the eggplant steaks and top with the coleslaw. Garnish with the scallions and jalapeños and serve with the pickled vegetables on the side.

ELOTE SALAD TOSTADAS

STREET CORN SALAD TOSTADA

MAKES 4

The Mexican word *elote* literally means "corn," a popular vegetable in Mexico that can be traced to the Aztecs. Today, corn on the cob served coated in butter, cotija cheese, mayonnaise, and chile powder is a popular street food. This recipe takes the kernels off the cob and serves them in a salad to enjoy on tostadas or in tacos.

1 cup (5¼ oz/150 g) cooked yellow corn kernels
2 tablespoons minced red onion
2 tablespoons diced tomato
1 tablespoon minced fresh jalapeño chile
2 tablespoons minced cucumber
¼ cup (2 fl oz/60 ml) Morita Mayonnaise (see page 31), or regular mayonnaise
Juice from 1 lime
Sea salt, to taste
4 corn or blue corn tortillas, 5 inches (13 cm) in diameter

Toppings
Chopped fresh cilantro (coriander)
Shredded cotija cheese or Parmesan
1 tablespoon chile-lime (Tajín) spice mix (see box)

Preheat the oven to 400°F (200°C/Gas mark 6).

In a mixing bowl, add the corn kernels with the red onion, tomato, jalapeño, cucumber, and the morita mayonnaise. Mix it all together, season with salt, then squeeze in the lime juice, season, and mix again.

To make the tostadas, bake the tortillas in the oven for 5 to 8 minutes on each side until golden and crispy; alternatively, pan fry them in vegetable oil. If you want to eat these as tacos, heat the tortillas in a comal or griddle (grill) pan.

Divide the corn salad between the tostadas and top with the cilantro, cotija cheese, and chile-lime powder.

Tajín seasoning is available as a prepared spice blend from Mexican stores and online retailers. Salty, tangy, and spicy, it is a blend of red chile powders, salt, citric acid, and dehydrated lime that is used as a fruit seasoning and general condiment. You can make your own by mixing chile or chipotle powder with dried lime zest and sea salt.

COLIFOR ROSTIZADA AL PASTOR

ROASTED CAULIFLOWER IN RED CHILE RUB

MAKES 10

The Spanish term *al pastor* means "shepherd style," and refers to how the main ingredient is marinated. Originally, the marinade was prepared for pork, inspired by a lamb dish brought to Mexico by Lebanese immigrants. Today, it is a popular street food in Mexico. In this recipe, you'll find the meat has been replaced with cauliflower, making a delicious vegan taco!

1 head cauliflower, trimmed
Vegetable oil

Marinade
3 guajillo chiles or 2 tablespoons smoked paprika
2 ancho chiles or 1 tablespoon chile powder
1 tablespoon garlic powder
1 tablespoon onion powder
1 tablespoon salt
1 teaspoon dried oregano
1 teaspoon ground cumin
½ cup (3 oz/85 g) diced pineapple
10 corn tortillas

Toppings
½ cup minced onion
1 cup (6 oz/175 g) diced pineapple
Chopped fresh cilantro (coriander)
Street Taco Salsa (see page 28)
Lime wedges

Make the marinade. If using the chiles, remove the stems (stalks) and seeds. Bring a deep saucepan of water to a boil over a high heat. Add the chiles, then turn off the heat, and let sit for about 10 minutes. Remove the chiles and reserve the water.

In a blender, add the chiles, spices and herbs, diced pineapple, and ⅓ cup (3 fl oz/90 ml) of the reserved water. Blend to a smooth mixture.

Slice the cauliflower in half from top to bottom, then slice it into ½-inch (12-mm)-thick steaks and put them into a resealable bag. Add the marinade, making sure the cauliflower is well covered, and let it sit for 30 minutes to an hour.

Heat a comal or flat griddle (grill) pan to a medium-high heat and brush all over with vegetable oil. Immediately add the cauliflower steaks with their marinade and sear for 3 to 5 minutes on each side.

Briefly heat the tortillas on a clean comal or flat griddle (grill) pan to warm them, then build the tacos, starting with a cauliflower steak and topping with onions, pineapple, and cilantro. Drizzle over the salsa and serve with lime wedges.

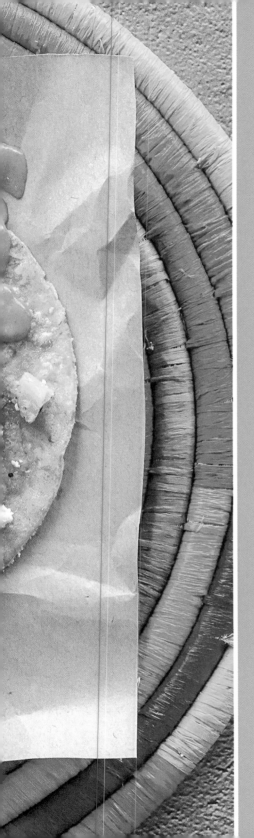

7

Healthy and Light

The recipes here are nutritionally well balanced and loaded with ingredients—such as cactus and purple yam—that are high in vitamins, minerals, antioxidants, and other known health benefits. There are also lighter options for those who want a less substantial meal.

Tacos don't have to be heavy or calorific. Reduce the amount of filling you put in your taco and pack it with shredded lettuce, cabbage, tomato, cucumber, radish, and other fresh raw ingredients. Leave off the cheese or substitute a low-fat version, or omit the tortilla and eat the fillings and toppings as a salad.

CARNE GUISADA

MEXICAN-STYLE BEEF STEW

MAKES 6

A simple, traditional slow-cooking beef stew flavored with cumin, jalapeños, and chile powder, this dish is popular throughout Latin America, especially in Puerto Rico and the Dominican Republic, and eaten as a taco filling along the Texas–Mexico border. This one has lean protein and it is cooked with vegetables that turn into a chunky salsa.

1 tablespoon avocado oil
1 lb (450 g) sirloin (rump) steak, cut into ½-inch (12-mm) cubes
1 teaspoon ground cumin
1 teaspoon dried oregano
1 teaspoon salt
½ large yellow (brown) onion, chopped
2 jalapeño chiles, chopped
1 cup diced (8 ½ oz/240 g) tomatoes with their juice
¼ cup (¾ oz/10 g) chopped cilantro (coriander)
6 corn or flour tortillas

Toppings
Queso fresco or feta cheese, crumbled
Homemade Red Salsa (see page 26)

Heat the oil in a Dutch oven or flameproof casserole dish over a high heat. When hot, add the beef, season with the cumin, oregano, and salt, and sear for 3 to 5 minutes, until browned.

Add the onion and chiles and sauté, stirring occasionally, for about 5 minutes, until the onion is translucent. Add the tomatoes with their juice, stir, cover, and reduce the heat. Let simmer for 25 minutes or until the beef is tender and the tomatoes break down into a sauce.

Meanwhile, briefly heat the tortillas on a comal or flat griddle (grill) pan to warm them, then build your taco, filling the tortillas with the stew, and adding the toppings.

VEGETALES ROSTIZADOS
ROASTED VEGETABLES

MAKES 8

A vegetable and bean recipe that is also vegetarian, these vegetable tacos are cooked with a very small amount of the plant-based cooking oil. Avocado oil is healthy, delicious, and has a light, fresh flavor. It also has a high smoking point at 500°F (260°C), which makes it the safest oil for high-heat cooking, such as searing and sautéing.

1 small sweet potato
1 large carrot
1 small yellow or orange bell pepper
½ small red onion
¼ small head cauliflower
¼ cup (1½ oz/40 g) cooked yellow corn kernels
1 teaspoon garlic powder
1 teaspoon smoked paprika
1 teaspoon freshly ground black pepper
Sea salt, to taste
2 tablespoons avocado oil
¼ cup cooked whole black beans
8 corn or blue corn tortillas

Toppings
Sliced scallions (spring onions)
Green salsa of your choice

Preheat the oven to 350°F (180°C/Gas Mark 4).

Cut the sweet potato, carrot, bell pepper, and onion into ¾-inch (2-cm) cubes and break the cauliflower into small pieces.

In a mixing bowl, add the vegetables and seasonings, then mix them all together well with the avocado oil, until evenly coated.

Transfer the vegetables to a roasting pan and roast in the preheated oven for about 15 minutes.

When the vegetables are ready, remove from the heat and mix in the black beans. Adjust seasoning as necessary. Briefly heat the tortillas on a comal or flat griddle (grill) pan to warm them, then build your taco, filling the tortillas with the vegetables and topping with scallions and green salsa.

TOSTADAS DE NOPALITOS

PRICKLY PEAR CACTUS PADDLE TOSTADA

MAKES 6

This salad features nopales, the cactus pads from the prickly pear cactus. Their meat-like texture has a mild flavor that resembles a mixture of asparagus and okra, both of which can be used as a substitute if you can't find nopales in supermarkets, Mexican grocery stores, or online.

1 cup (3 oz/85 g) diced nopales, from a jar
½ cup (2½ oz/70 g) halved cherry tomatoes
¼ cup (1 oz/25 g) minced jalapeño chiles
½ cup (2 oz/60 g) minced red onion
¼ cup (¾ oz/10 g) chopped fresh cilantro (coriander)
¼ cup (1 oz/30 g) diced jícama or radish
1 teaspoon dried oregano
Juice of 1 lime
1 tablespoon olive oil
6 corn tortillas, 5 inches (13 cm) in diameter
Sea salt and freshly ground black pepper, to taste

Toppings
Sliced avocado or Guacamole (see page 54)
Pickled Red Onions (see page 56)

Preheat the oven to 400°F (200°C/Gas mark 6).

In a mixing bowl, add the nopales, cherry tomatoes, jalapeño chiles, red onion, cilantro (coriander), and jícama or radish. Then add the dried oregano, lime juice, and olive oil, and season with salt and black pepper. Mix together until the vegetables are well coated with the seasonings.

To make tostadas, bake the tortillas in the oven for 5 to 8 minutes on each side until golden and crispy (or pan fry them).

Fill the tostadas with the salad and top with sliced avocado or guacamole and picked red onions.

Jícama is also known as the Mexican potato, Mexican yam, and Mexican turnip, along with a few other names. The only part that is eaten is the tuber, which looks like a brown beet from the outside, resembles a potato inside, but tastes more like a cross between an apple and water chestnut. If you struggle to find it, substitute white daikon (mooli) radish or Jerusalem artichoke for eating raw, but if the recipe calls for heat, water chestnuts are a better substitute.

POLLO TROPICANO
TROPICAL CHICKEN

MAKES 6

The bright sunshiny sweetness of pineapple creates a light, juicy chicken taco that is perfect as a quick summertime meal. Native to the tropical areas of Mexico, Caribbean, and Central and South America, pineapples are thought to have been cultivated by the Mayas and Aztecs since 750 BCE.

2 skinless, boneless chicken breasts
1 tablespoon avocado oil
1 teaspoon garlic powder
1 teaspoon chile powder
6 corn tortillas
Sea salt and freshly ground black
    pepper, to taste

Toppings
1 cup (8 fl oz/240 ml) Pineapple Pico
    de Gallo (see page 38)
Chopped fresh coriander (cilantro)
Morita Mayonnaise (see page 31)
Queso fresco or feta cheese, crumbled
Lime wedges

Rub the chicken all over with the oil, garlic powder, chile powder, and salt and pepper.

Heat a lidded skillet or frying pan over a high heat. When hot, place the chicken breasts in the pan and sear for about 1 minute until the bottom is browned, then turn over, reduce the heat to medium, and cover. Let cook for 10 to 15 minutes. Check occasionally, and if the chicken seems dry, add a tablespoon of water and cover again so that the steam helps to moisten the meat.

When cooked, remove the chicken breasts from the pan and transfer to a cutting (chopping) board. Let rest for 3 minutes, then slice into ½-inch (12-mm)-thick strips.

Briefly heat the tortillas on a comal or flat griddle (grill) pan to warm them, then build your taco, filling the tortillas with the chicken and topping with the pineapple pico de gallo, queso fresco, a drizzle of morita mayonnaise and a squeeze of lime.

PICADILLO DE PAVO
TURKEY STIR-FRY

MAKES 12

Spanish picadillo recipes featuring ground meat have been adopted by
Mexican cooks, who've added their native ingredients, influenced by the
regions in which they live. In the north, ancho chile is a favorite, while raisins
or other fruit are popular in the south. Here's my take on it: a vegetable-
packed recipe using lean ground turkey for a healthier option.

2 tablespoons vegetable oil
1 lb (450 g) ground (minced) turkey
½ large yellow (brown) onion, minced
3 cloves garlic, peeled and minced
¼ cup (1 oz/30 g) diced jalapeño chiles
½ small yellow bell pepper, diced
½ small red bell pepper, diced
½ carrot, diced
½ cup (2¼ oz/65 g) diced sweet potato
½ cup (2¼ oz/65 g) chopped
  cauliflower
1 cup (8 fl oz/240 ml) vegetable broth
  (stock)
1 cup (8½ oz/240 g) diced tomatoes
⅓ cup (2 oz/55 g) cooked yellow corn
  kernels
1 teaspoon dried oregano
1 teaspoon ground cumin
1 cup (1 oz/30 g) spinach
12 corn or flour tortillas
Sea salt and freshly ground black
  pepper, to taste

Toppings
Avocado slices
Cooked red bell pepper slice

Heat the oil in a skillet or frying pan over a high heat. When hot,
add the ground turkey and break it down with a wooden spoon.
Let it sear for 2 to 3 minutes, until browned, then transfer to a
separate container and set aside.

In the same pan, sauté the onion, garlic, jalapeños, bell pepper,
carrot, sweet potato, and cauliflower, stirring occasionally, for
3 to 5 minutes, until the vegetables start to soften.

Deglaze with the vegetable broth (stock). When it starts to
simmer, reduce the heat to medium, and add the turkey,
tomatoes, and corn. Season with oregano, cumin, salt, and
pepper, and simmer for 10 minutes or until the sweet potatoes
are soft. Fold in the spinach at the very end.

Briefly heat the tortillas on a comal or flat griddle (grill) pan to
warm them, then fill them with the picadillo mixture. Top with
avocado slices and red bell pepper.

PAPA MORADA Y VEGANO CHORIZO

PURPLE POTATO AND VEGAN CHORIZO

MAKES 6

The vividly colored purple yam is high in fibre, potassium, vitamin C, and antioxidants. Research even suggests that the two anthocyanins in purple yams—cyanidin and peonidin—may reduce the growth of certain types of cancers. Purple sweet potatoes are also highly nutrition, but are a bit less sweet and more calorific than the yams.

2 tablespoons avocado oil
1 cup (5¼ oz/150 g) diced purple yam
   or sweet potato
½ red onion, diced
1 large orange bell pepper, diced
1 large poblano pepper, diced
¼ cup (1 oz/30 g) vegan chorizo
6 corn or flour tortillas

Toppings
Sliced radish
Chopped fresh coriander (cilantro)

Heat the oil in a cast-iron skillet or frying pan set over a medium-high heat. When hot, add the yam or sweet potato and sauté for about 5 minutes, until seared on all sides.

Add the onion, bell pepper, and poblano pepper, and sauté for about 5 minutes, until the onion is translucent.

Move the vegetables to the sides of the pan to create a hole in the middle, then add the chorizo to the center and cook, stirring occasionally, for about 2 to 3 minutes, until browned and crumbled.

Mix the vegetables in with the chorizo, reduce the heat to medium, cover, and let cook, stirring occasionally, for 6 to 10 minutes. If the yams are still hard and dry, add a tablespoon of water and cover again. Repeat until the yams are soft.

Briefly heat the tortillas on a comal or flat griddle (grill) pan to warm them, then fill with the yams. Top with radish for a nice crunch and sprinkle over cilantro.

TOSTADA DE SALPICÓN

SHREDDED BEEF SALAD TOSTADA

MAKES 8

Salpicón is a refreshing Mexican salad. This version is made with shredded beef, but you could also make it with chicken or fish.

. . . .

1 lb (450 g) beef brisket, skirt, or other cut suitable for shredding
¼ white onion
2 cloves garlic, peeled
1 tablespoon salt
1 bay leaf
½ cup (4 oz/115 g) diced tomatoes
½ small red onion, thinly sliced
½ cup (1¾ oz/50 g) sliced cucumbers
¼ cup (¾ oz/10 g) chopped fresh cilantro (coriander)
¼ cup (1 oz/30 g) sliced radishes
Sea salt and freshly ground black pepper, to taste

Dressing
½ cup (4 fl oz/120 ml) olive oil
3 tablespoons apple cider vinegar
2 tablespoons lime juice
1 tablespoon dried oregano
8 corn tortillas, 5 inches (13 cm) in diameter

Toppings
Shredded red cabbage
Shredded romaine lettuce
Pickled Red Onions (see page 56)
Fresh coriander (cilantro) leaves
Street Taco Salsa (see page 28)

Add the brisket to a deep pot and fill it up with enough water to cover the meat. Add the white onion, garlic, salt, and bay leaf. Bring to a boil, then reduce heat and let simmer for about 2 hours or until meat is tender.

When the beef is cooked, remove it from the pot, then shred it using two forks (or let it cool for a few minutes and shred with your hands). Preheat the oven to 400°F (200°C/Gas mark 6).

Add the shredded beef to a mixing bowl and toss in the tomato, red onion, cucumber, cilantro, and radishes. Season with salt and black pepper.

For the dressing, in a separate small bowl, add the oil, apple cider vinegar, lime juice, oregano, and salt and pepper to taste, then whisk until you form a vinaigrette. Pour it over the shredded beef salad.

To make tostadas, bake the tortillas in the oven for 5 to 8 minutes on each side until golden and crispy (or pan fry them).

Layer the salad on top of tostadas and top with the cabbage, lettuce, pickled red onion, and cilantro. Drizzle over the salsa.

CALABACITAS Y QUINOA

SQUASH AND QUINOA

MAKES 6

Pronounced "keen-wa," quinoa is used like a grain but is actually a seed. It formed part of a staple diet for the Incas thousands of years ago, and has become popular as a healthier alternative to rice. It can be layered in these vegetarian tacos or added to the stew.

2 tablespoons vegetable oil
¼ onion, chopped
1 jalapeño chile, minced
1 calabacita or zucchini (courgette), diced
1 teaspoon dried oregano
½ cup (2½ oz/70 g) halved cherry tomatoes
¼ cup (1½ oz/40 g) cooked yellow corn kernels
1 cup (1 oz/30 g) spinach `
1 cup (6 oz/185 g) cooked quinoa
6 corn tortillas
Sea salt and freshly ground black pepper, to taste
Queso fresco or feta cheese, cubed
2 sprigs fresh cilantro (coriander), chopped

Sauce
½ cup (4 fl oz/120 ml) vegetable broth (stock)
2 tomatoes
¼ onion
2 cloves garlic, peeled and minced

To make the tomato sauce, add the vegetable broth (stock), tomatoes, onion, and garlic to a blender or food processor and blend until smooth.

Add the oil to a skillet or frying pan set over a medium-high heat. Swirl it around and, when hot, add the chopped onion and jalapeño. Sauté, stirring occasionally, for about 3 minutes, until the onion is translucent.

Add the calabacita or zucchini, followed by the tomato sauce, then season with oregano and reduce the heat to medium. When it starts to simmer, add the cherry tomatoes and corn kernels, then heat for 5 minutes. Turn the heat off and stir in the spinach. Add the quinoa to the stew or layer separately in the tacos.

Briefly heat the tortillas on a comal or flat griddle (grill) pan to warm them, then fill with the stew and top with queso fresco or feta cheese cubes and cilantro.

8

Taco Party!

Who doesn't love tacos, especially when combined with a fiesta? Let's get down to it and feed a crowd in no time!

Here are ways to size up your recipes and serve a lot of guests at once. There are slow-cooking recipes that you can start early in the day, stews that can be made in big pots, and grilled meat that you can cook and serve outside.

The beauty about having a taco party is that so many of the toppings can be prepared ahead and laid out on a buffet or picnic table for guests to create their tacos exactly as they like them.

ENCHILADAS POTOSINAS

CENTRAL MEXICAN RED ENCHILADAS

MAKES 20–24

These enchiladas may look more like empanadas, because the tortillas are folded, not rolled, but they are made with masa harina instead of wheat flour. The recipe was thought to have originated in the early 1900 in the state of San Luis Potosís when chile particles were accidentally left in the mill during the grinding of corn for masa harina. The red-colored chile flour was then used in local recipes.

Vegetable oil, for frying

Dough
2 ancho chiles or ½ tablespoon chile powder
3 cups (12 oz/350 g) masa harina (corn flour)
1 tablespoon salt
1½ cups (12 fl oz/350 ml) lukewarm water

Filling
3 tomatillos
1 jalapeño chile, chopped
2 cups crumbled queso fresco or feta cheese
½ onion, minced

Toppings
Shredded cabbage
Pico de gallo (see box page 38)
Chopped fresh cilantro (coriander)
Mexican crema or sour cream
Queso fresco or feta cheese, crumbled

Make the dough. Put the dried ancho chiles into a mixing bowl and add enough hot water to cover. Let them soak for about 20 minutes. When soft, blend with 1 cup of water to form a paste.

In a large mixing bowl, add the masa harina (corn flour), salt, a little of the lukewarm water, and the chile paste. Mix together, and, adding a little water at a time, start to knead until the dough is soft and has the desired red color. Make sure the dough is not too dry or sticky. When you obtain the desired consistency, let it rest for 10 minutes.

Meanwhile, prepare the filling. Pulse blend the tomatillos and jalapeño chile to a chunky consistency and strain.

In a mixing bowl, add the cheese, the tomatillo–jalapeño relish, and the minced onion. Mix until well combined. Set aside.

Start forming 20 to 24 small balls with the dough. Keep them moist by placing damp kitchen paper towels over them.

Using a tortilla press or two heavy, flat objects, press each dough ball between two square sheets of parchment (baking paper) to make the tortillas (see pages 46–7).

Place a tortilla in a nonstick skillet or frying pan or on a lightly oiled comal or griddle (grill) pan over a medium heat, then add a

small scoop of the queso fresco filling on one side and carefully fold over the other side to make a semi-circle. Press the edges with a spatula to seal.

Cook for 30 seconds, then carefully flip over to the other side and cook for another 30 seconds. Transfer to a tray and quickly repeat for the remaining tortillas.

When ready to serve, heat a skillet with enough vegetable oil to cover the surface and fry the enchiladas on both sides, then place them on a cooling rack. Add the shredded cabbage, pico de gallo, cilantro, and drizzle over Mexican crema or sour cream.

DISCADA

MIXED MEATS

MAKES 20–30

A combination of grilled meats is included in this popular north Mexican dish, which takes its name from the *discada*, a round iron or steel disk with a similar shape to a Chinese wok, which is used to cook it. The center remains hot for cooking while the cooler edges keep cooked food warm.

2 tablespoons vegetable oil
4 thick slices (rashers) bacon, chopped
4 oz (115 g) chorizo, crumbled
1 lb (450 g) pork, chopped
1 lb (450 g) ribeye or flank (beef) steak, chopped
8 oz (225 g) smoked sausages, chopped
1 large yellow (brown) onion, diced
1 red bell pepper, diced
2 jalapeño chiles, diced
1 cup (8 fl oz/240 ml) Mexican beer
2 tomatoes, diced
1 teaspoon garlic powder
1 teaspoon ground cumin
20–30 corn or flour tortillas
Sea salt and freshly ground black pepper, to taste

Toppings
Fresh cilantro (coriander) leaves
Minced onion
Street Taco Salsa (see page 28)
Lime wedges

Heat the oil in a discada, a large cast-iron skillet, or a frying pan over a medium heat. Add the bacon and cook for a few minutes until crispy, then transfer to a separate container with a slotted spoon to retain as much fat as possible in the pan.

In the same pan, cook the chorizo and again remove it with a slotted spoon to retain as much of the fat as possible.

Now sear the pork on all sides, remove it, and set aside. It's fine if it isn't yet completely cooked. Repeat the same process with the beef and sausages.

Still in the same pan, add the onion, pepper, and jalapeños, and sauté, stirring occasionally, for about 5 minutes, until the onion starts to caramelize. Add all the cooked meats back to the pan and deglaze with the beer. When the mixture starts to simmer, add the tomatoes, garlic powder, and ground cumin, and season with salt and black pepper. Cook for 20 minutes or until the meats are soft.

Heat the tortillas on a comal or flat griddle (grill) pan. Serve the mixed meats with the warm tortillas and toppings.

> It is important to cook each of the meats separately to ensure they have a nice sear on them and are cooked with the right texture—a crisp exterior with a soft interior—you want to avoid them becoming mushy when you add them all back together in the pan.

BARBACOA
SLOW-ROASTED BEEF

MAKES 20

Traditionally made with lamb or goat, this recipe hails from Mexico and the Caribbean. The meat is cooked slowly until tender, succulent, and easy to shred with two forks. You can also use it to fill burritos, enchiladas, and quesadillas.

3 lbs (1.4 kg) chuck roast (braising steak)
3 lbs (1.4 kg) beef cheek (if you can't find beef cheek, use double the quantity of chuck roast)
3 cups (1¼ pints/700 ml) beef broth (stock)
1 yellow (brown) onion
4 cloves garlic, peeled
1 tablespoon ground cumin
1 tablespoon dried oregano
1 tablespoon salt
1½ teaspoons freshly ground black pepper
3 bay leaves
2 dried chiles de árbol or Thai (bird's eye) chiles
Sea salt and freshly ground black pepper
20 tortillas

Toppings
Fresh cilantro (coriander) leaves
Minced onions
Stone Mortar Salsa (see page 30)
Lime wedges

Preheat the oven to 350°F (180°C/Gas Mark 4).

Cut the two types of beef into large chunks, a little smaller than the palm of your hand, and season with salt and black pepper.

Heat a large skillet or frying pan over a high heat. When hot, start browning the meat on all sides—you may need to do this in batches. Transfer all the meat to a large Dutch oven or deep casserole dish.

In a blender, add the beef broth (stock), onion, garlic, cumin, oregano, salt, and pepper and blend until smooth.

Pour the broth mixture over the meat, add bay leaves and chiles de árbol, and cover. Cook in the preheated oven for 3 to 4 hours. The barbacoa is ready when the beef shreds easily. Remove and discard the bay leaves.

Heat the tortillas on a comal or flat griddle (grill) pan. Serve the barbacoa with the tortillas and cilantro (coriander), onions, salsa, lime wedges, and any other toppings or side dishes you like.

This is a great recipe for a slow cooker, if you have one. After browning the beef, transfer the meat to the slow cooker. Pour the beef broth mixture over the meat and cook for 8 to 9 hours.

CARNITAS
BRAISED PORK

MAKES 20

Carnitas means "little meats" and refers to the strands of pulled pork that are crispy on the outside but soft inside. The style may vary from region to region, but the tacos are enjoyed throughout Mexico, often on festive occasions and Sundays at the traditional *mercado*, or "marketplace."

· ·

4 lbs (1.8 kg) pork butt (shoulder)
2 cups (1 lb/450 g) pork fat
1 cup (8 fl oz/240 ml) vegetable oil
1 yellow (brown) onion, cut into 1-inch
    (2.5-cm) slices
8 cloves garlic, peeled and minced
1 orange, peeled and cut into thick slices
Sea salt and freshly ground black
    pepper
20 corn or flour tortillas

Toppings
Fresh cilantro (coriander) leaves
Minced onions
Guacamole (see page 54)
Serrano-Cucumber Salsa (see page 36)
Lime wedges

Cut the pork into large chunks and season with salt and pepper.

Heat the pork fat and oil in a deep pot over a high heat. Carefully start to add the pork and fry the chunks on all sides for 10 to 15 minutes, until they turn a golden brown. Reduce the heat to medium and continue cooking for 10 to 20 minutes; if the heat is too high and creating a lot of bubbles, lower the temperature.

Add the onion, garlic, and orange slices, and simmer for another 20 minutes or until the meat is soft and shreds easily. Remove the carnitas with a slotted spoon and shred them with a fork.

Heat the tortillas on a comal or flat griddle (grill) pan. Serve the carnitas with the warm tortillas, cilantro, onions, guacamole, salsa, lime wedges, and any other toppings or side dishes you like, so people can serve themselves.

DORADOS DE PAPA
CRISPY POTATO

MAKES 20

**Dorados means "golden," the color of these tacos after
being filled and fried. The recipe uses mashed potatoes, a popular
filling in Mexico, to make a vegetarian option for your party.**

8 russet (King Edward) potatoes, boiled,
    peeled, and mashed
1 tablespoon chipotle purée or paste,
    or to taste
1 teaspoon ground cumin
1 teaspoon garlic powder
1 teaspoon onion powder
2 teaspoons salt
1 teaspoon ground black pepper
20 corn tortillas
Vegetable oil, for frying

Toppings
Avocado Crema (see page 32)
Pico de gallo (see box page 38)
Queso fresco or feta cheese, crumbled

In a mixing bowl, add the mashed potatoes, chipotle purée, cumin, garlic powder, onion powder, salt, and pepper. Mix together until well combined. Taste and adjust the seasoning, if necessary.

Stacking 10 tortillas at a time, cover them with a clean kitchen towel and microwave for 1 minute.

Pile a scoop of potato mixture on one side of a tortilla, fold the other side over, and press lightly to close. Do not press the edges together to seal! If you find the filling escaping, you may like to secure the edge with a toothpick (cocktail stick). Repeat for all the tortillas.

Add oil to a wide skillet or frying pan until about ¼ inch (6 mm) deep. Heat over a high heat. When hot, fry the dorados until crispy on both sides, about 2 minutes.

Serve with the avocado crema, pico de gallo, and cheese.

BIRRIA DE RES
RED BEEF STEW

MAKES 20–30

Traditionally, birria is a stew based on goat meat and cooked over low heat in an *olla*, or "pot," but you could cook it in a slow cooker, too. It is a favorite in central Mexico, but there are street carts and restaurants, known as *birrierias*, that serve the dish throughout the country. This recipe uses beef as a substitute for the goat, but lamb could be used.

10 guajillo chiles, stems and seeds removed
2 ancho chiles, stems and seeds removed
6 chiles de árbol, stems and seeds removed
8 cups (3½ pints/2 liters) beef broth (stock)
¼ cup (2 fl oz/60 ml) apple cider vinegar
6 cloves garlic, peeled
1 onion, quartered
½ tablespoon ground cumin
1 teaspoon ground cinnamon
½ teaspoon ground cloves
1 tablespoon minced ginger
5 lbs (2.2 kg) boneless beef chuck roast (stewing steak)
5 lbs (2.2 kg) beef shank (shin of beef)
20–30 tortillas
Vegetable oil, for frying
Sea salt and freshly ground black pepper, to taste

Toppings
Fresh cilantro (coriander) leaves
Minced onion
Homemade Roasted Tomatillo Salsa (see page 27)
Lime wedges

Preheat the oven to 350°F (180°C/Gas Mark 4).

In a deep pot, add 4 cups (1¾ pints/1 liter) of water and bring to a boil. Add the dried chiles and cook until soft. Let cool and strain.

Blend the drained chiles with the beef broth (stock), vinegar, garlic, onion, cumin, cinnamon, cloves, ginger, salt, and pepper.

Add enough oil to coat a large skillet or frying pan over a high heat. When hot, sear the meat chunks for about 5 minutes on each side, until browned. You may have to work in batches.

When browned, transfer the meat to a Dutch oven or deep casserole dish.

Pour over the birria broth (stock), then seal with aluminum foil to keep in the moisture and cover with a lid. Place in the preheated oven for 3 to 5 hours.

Heat the tortillas on a comal or flat griddle (grill) pan. Serve the birria with the warm tortillas and cilantro, onions, salsa, and lime wedges.

FLAUTAS DE POLLO
CHICKEN FLAUTAS

MAKES 20–30

Flautas, which means "whistle" or "flute," are rolled tortillas filled with meat and fried. The tube shape is ideal for holding in the shredded chicken but you can, of course, use meat to make tacos instead.

5 lbs (2.3 kg) chicken breasts
½ yellow (brown) onion
4 cloves garlic, peeled
2 bay leaves
20–30 corn tortillas
1 cup (8 fl oz/240 ml) vegetable oil,
    for frying, plus extra
Sea salt and freshly ground black
    pepper, to taste

Toppings
Shredded lettuce
Chopped tomato
Sliced red onion
Queso fresco or feta cheese, crumbled
Homemade Red Salsa (see page 26)
Avocado Crema (see page 32)

In a deep pot over a high heat, add the chicken breasts and enough water to cover the meat. Add the onion, garlic, bay leaves, salt, and pepper, and bring to a boil. Reduce the heat to medium-high and simmer for 15 to 20 minutes or until cooked. Remove the breasts from the water and let cool.

Shred the chicken into thin strips using two forks or your fingers.

Heat tortillas in stacks of 10 in the microwave for 1 minute, then cover them in a clean damp kitchen towel to make sure they don't dry out.

Place about 2 tablespoons of shredded chicken close to one edge of a tortilla and roll it as tight as possible. Insert a toothpick across the flauta on a diagonal angle to hold it together. Continue to roll flautas until you have used all the chicken filling.

Heat the vegetable oil in a large skillet or frying pan set over a medium-high heat. When hot, add a few flautas at a time and cook for 3 to 5 minutes, until they are crisp on both sides, using tongs to turn them. Add more oil as needed. Transfer the flautas to a cooling rack or a tray with lined with kitchen paper towels.

Serve with the toppings.

You'll need enough toothpicks (cocktail sticks) to seal the tortillas before frying. You'll also need enough vegetable oil for frying multiple batches. Choose one with a neutral flavor that is suitable for high frying temperatures, such as sunflower oil or canola (rapeseed) oil—make sure you discard it once the oil starts getting too brown.

SHOPPING RESOURCES

USA

AMIGO FOODS

www.amigofoods.com

An online supplier selling imported Mexican food and drinks, including canned and packaged goods, such as flour, rice, hot sauces and condiments, beans, chiles, tomatillos, chiles in adobo, mole, crema, purées and pastes, and salsas.

COCHINITACO

www.cochinitaco.com

Victoria Elizondo's kitchen at Kickin' Kombucha in Houston offers vibrant Mexican food made from scratch, with unique ingredients from local vendors. Open for breakfast, brunch, lunch, and dinner, you can also order online. The Cochinita & Co. market sells tamales, totopos, plus a range of salsas, guacamole, and trail mix.

EL MILAGRO

el-milagro.com

El Milagro is a family-owned tortilla company that started in 1950 in Chicago, Illinois, manufacturing the highest-quality tortilla products, which are fresh, authentic, made without GMO or preservatives, and use traditional processes.

MEXGROCER

www.mexgrocer.com   www.mexgrocer.co.uk

This international company specializes in authentic Mexican groceries and ingredients such as chiles, beans, rice, nopales (prickly pear cactus), and desserts, including vegan and vegetarian options. A good range of tortilla presses and warmers, as well as molcajetes, and party decorations.

MY MEXICO MARKET

www.mymexicostore.com

An online merchant for everything Mexican, it sells canned, preserved, and dry goods, including rice, beans, tortillas, and tamales; chiles, sauces, salsas, mole, and condiments; snacks and sweet things; and a vast range of Mexican cookware.

WORLD MARKET

www.worldmarket.com

A destination for international gourmet food and hard-to-find global products, this online supplier stocks a wide range of Mexican products, including condiments, seasonings, snacks, sauces, canned and preserved ingredients, and drinks.

ZOCALO FOODS

www.zocalofoods.com

Buy basics like flour, rice, and beans, condiments and seasonings, and canned fruit and vegetables (chiles, nopales, tomatillos, soups, and stews), sauces and salsas, as well as popular snacks, candy, cookies, and desserts.

UK

COOL CHILE

www.coolchile.co.uk

As their name suggests, this site sells Mexican chiles, powders, herbs and spices, as well as all types of Mexican storecupboard essentials. The specialty is their white and blue corn tortillas, made fresh daily in London, and available in sizes ranging from tiny bite-sized versions at $2\frac{1}{2}$ inches (6 cm) in diameter to giants at $7\frac{3}{4}$ inches (20 cm).

LA TIENDITA

LaTiendita.co.uk

Here you can buy Mexican groceries from over 20 well-known brands including Tajín. You will find tomatillos, mole, chile in adobo, and a wide range of dried chiles and tortillas as well cookware.

MESTIZO MARKET

mestizomarket.com

The market website of the popular Hampstead, London, restaurant and tequila bar stocks fresh and frozen food so you can pick up taco fillings (tinga, pibil, and al pastor), queso, chicharrones, chorizo, tortillas, and tamales.

MEXICAN MAMA

mexican-mama.com

An authentic Mexican supermarket in London supplying homemade tamales and ready meals, as well as sweet pastries, and chiles, sauces, snacks, canned goods, condiments, herbs and spices, flours, tortillas, and marinades.

AUSTRALIA

CHILE MOJO

www.chilemojo.com.au

An American and Australian couple started this company and sell their own Mexican spice blends, as well as groceries, dried chiles and chile powders, fresh food, drinks, and handcrafted artisan gifts. They claim to have the largest hot sauce selection in the country. Order online or go to their store in St Morris, South Australia.

EL CIELO

elcielo.com.au

The company uses Australian-grown corn combined with traditional Mexican processes to make their corn tortillas and chips. Choose from fresh tortillas, corn chips, chile sauces, beans, corn masa flour, dried chiles, and meal kit boxes.

FIREWORKS FOODS

fireworksfoods.com.au

A one-stop shop for dried chiles, salsas, tortillas, hot sauces, herbs and spices, pastes and purées, tomatillos, nopales (cactus), cheese moles, flour, as well as cookware, craftware, tableware, and piñatas.

POBLANO MEXICAN

poblanomexican.com.au

One of the largest suppliers of Mexican food, you can buy their products online or at their warehouse itself in Cheltenham. They deliver refrigerated and frozen foods by van, within 15 km of Melbourne. Along with the usual canned and dried Mexican ingredients, tortillas, flours, chiles, herbs and spices, pastes, sauces, cheese, sausages, chorizo, and condiments, they specialize in more unusual and hard-to-find imported Mexican products.

NEW ZEALAND

AYACARAMBA

www.aycaramba.co.nz

Shop here for chiles, salsas, seasonings, pastes and purées, beans and other canned goods, snacks, sweet things, drinks, and a big range of tortillas including flour, blue, yellow, white corn, and cactus.

MEXI FOODS

www.mexifoods.co.nz   www.mexibev.co.nz

Here you can find chiles dried or in jars and cans, pastes and powders, mole, sauces, condiments, herbs, spices, and seasonings, and cookware.

TIO PABLO

www.tiopablo.co.nz

Stocking their own products as well as the La Morena brand, there are authentic Mexican groceries and ingredients, such as corn tortillas, tostadas, tortilla chips, salsas, chiles, masa harina, tomatillos, cactus, nuts and seeds, meal kits, and more.

INDEX

ACKNOWLEDGMENTS

This book is dedicated to my mom. She taught me to be persistent, to work hard, and to let my imagination run wild. I would also like to thank my business partner Robert Lopez for giving us an opportunity when we needed it the most. Our partnership has turned into one of the best eateries in Houston, Texas, and because of it, more doors continue to open for us. I would also like to thank my staff, Enedina, Adrian, Pedro, Carlos, and my mother, Graciela, for helping me make this possible by working extra hours and being supportive of this project. Lastly to my friend, Valerie: Thank you for not only photographing this book, but for your constant support and friendship.

PICTURE CREDITS

© Welbeck Non-Fiction Limited: 17, 18–19, 26–7, 29, 31, 33, 35, 36, 39, 42, 44, 47, 51, 53, 55, 57, 59, 61, 62, 65, 67, 71, 73, 75, 77, 81, 83, 85, 89, 91, 93, 95, 96, 99, 101, 105, 107, 111, 113, 114–5, 117, 119, 121, 123, 125, 129, 131, 133, 134, 137, 139, 141, 145, 147, 149, 151, 153, 154–5, 157, 159, 161, 163, 165, 167, 169. Getty Images: 21 4kodiak, 87 Westend61, 108 Nik West, 109 James Gritz. Shutterstock: 13 Marcos Castillo, 23 Rawpixel.com, 45 Anna Williams Images, 40–1 Hulevskyy Volodymyr. Unsplash: 9 Daniel Lloyd Blunk Fernandez; 10 reiseuhu; 14 Miranda Garside; 16 Roberto Carlos Román Don; 34 Yethu Mtshali; 37 Shelley Pauls; 49–9 Erik Dungan; 68–9 Nick Fewings; 86 Rafael Hoyos; 126–7 Victor Figueroa; 142–3 Jorge Zapata. Victoria Elizondo: 5,6 / Trish Badger, 7, 12l, 12r, 13, 78, 102, 176 / Shawn Chippendale.